All About
UPSC
Civil Services Exam

Another Important Book By Same Author

ESSAYS DEMYSTIFIED

for UPSC CSE *& Competitive Exams*

Nishant Jain, IAS
Abhishek Saraf, IAS
Snehil Tripathi

All About UPSC Civil Services Exam

Nishant Jain, IAS

Published by

PRABHAT PRAKASHAN PVT. LTD.
4/19 Asaf Ali Road,
New Delhi-110 002 (INDIA)
e-mail: prabhatbooks@gmail.com

ISBN 978-93-5266-557-0

ALL ABOUT UPSC CIVIL SERVICES EXAM
Translation by: Harish Jain

Edition
2026

Price
₹ 395 (Rupees Three Hundred Ninety Five Only)

Printed at: Yash Printographics, Noida

Karmanyevadhikaarastey ma phaleshu kadachana.
Ma karmaphalhetubhurwah ma te sangotsva karmaani.
—Shrimad Bhagvad Gita

Parasparopgraho Jeevanam
—Tatvartha Sutra

"The Woods are Lovely, dark and deep,
But I have promises to keep,
And miles to go before I sleep,
And miles to go before I sleep."
—Robert Frost

"The cold breeze does come from the current of this river,
Although the boat is feeble, but it challenges the waves.
Go and find a spark from somewhere my friends,
There is still some zeal left in you, try to light it".
—Dushyant Kumar

Commendations

In 2016, I got an opportunity to deliver a motivational talk at the Lal Bahadur Shastri National Academy of Administration, the training centre of I.A.S. officers. There, I met Mr. Nishant Jain, the author of this book.

This young I.A.S. officer was co-ordinating and conducting the programme proficiently. I was exalted to know that Nishant had secured the 13th rank in the Civil Services Examination, 2014, UPSC and topped the exam from the Hindi medium.

After meeting him, I felt that such talented people pave their own way by dint of their simplicity, brio, confidence and positivity as well as motivate and lead others by their deeds.

After reading his views and knowing his thoughts on 'Joy of Giving', I got more acquainted with his personality. I feel that those, who are born to do good deeds, lead their lives with responsibility. It is because of the realization of this responsibility that Nishant Jain, after becoming a topper, has decided to present the gist of his knowledge, understanding and experience in the form of this book, and thereby enabling the I.A.S. aspirants to get benefitted by the book.

Millions of Indians dream to succeed and top in the examination of Indian Civil Services. It is neither easy nor impossible. The book by Nishant Jain 'All about UPSC Civil Services Exam', will positively guide the aspirants of Civil Services in their journey towards achieving their dreams.

I congratulate him on his unprecedented and sensitive task, and wish him success in all his endeavors.

—Kailash Kher

(Noted Sufi singer and Lyricist and Padmashree Awardee)

❍❍❍

Every year, millions of aspirants dream to become an I.A.S. and I.P.S. officer. With utmost dedication, they prepare and try their level best to crack the exam; but sometimes, the desired results are not achieved due to the lack of a proper and relevant guidance and confidence,. Nishant Jain, the author of this book, studied in the Hindi medium and made history by securing the 13th rank in I.A.S. examination. Such an ideal example boosts up the morale of the aspirants. Nishant's indomitable spirit and his desire to 'achieve something great' can be clearly seen in his book. I firmly believe that this book will definitely help in clearing the doubts of the aspirants of Civil Services. My best Wishes.

—Anand Kumar

(Well known educationist and the founder of 'Super 30')

❍❍❍

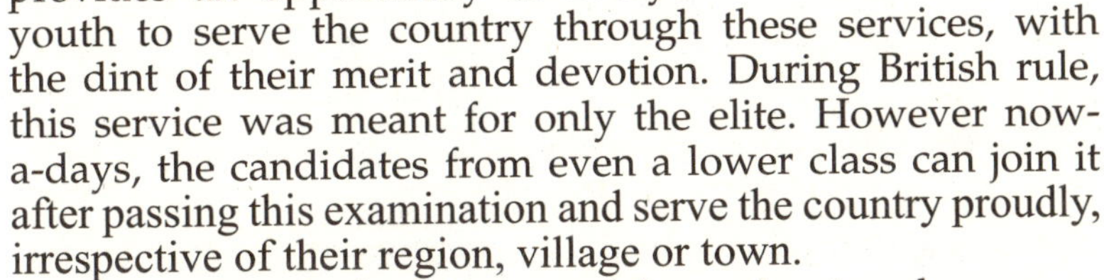

The examination of Indian Civil Services (I.C.S.) was started during the British period. The selection process for this all India Competitive Examination was designed with the objective to make the functioning of law and order smooth in India.

After Independence, the Indian Civil Services is known as the Indian Administrative Service. The Constitution of India provides an opportunity to every youth to serve the country through these services, with the dint of their merit and devotion. During British rule, this service was meant for only the elite. However now-a-days, the candidates from even a lower class can join it after passing this examination and serve the country proudly, irrespective of their region, village or town.

As we know, a large group of the aspirants, who appear in this examination, speak, write and think in Hindi and Indian languages; Medium of any Indian language is not and should not be a hurdle. The only basis of selection is talent and ability in the Indian Civil Services; and ability lies in each and every person.

The excellent performance of Nishant Jain in the examination has allayed the fear of such aspirants that they cannot get good ranks in I.A.S. examination through their own language. Hence, he should be lauded for not only presenting an ideal example to these aspirants but also guiding them through his experiences compiled in the form of this book.

I find it an inspirational gift from Nishant Jain, dedicated to those aspirants who feel proud in speaking and writing in their mother tongue.

Congratulations and best wishes!

—Malini Awasthi

(Padmashree Awardee, Famous Folk Singer)

OOO

This book, for the Civil Services Examination, covers all the important aspects. The interesting fact, that Nishant takes the help of some poems, proverbs and sayings to express his own views in this book, will definitely help the readers to remain interested in the book. This book is a motivational book filled with positivity, which will help greatly in preparing for the Civil Services examination.
My best wishes.

—Gaurav Agrawal
IAS, Rank 1, UPSC-2013

❍❍❍

Non availability of guidance for CSE is no longer a problem these days. However, referring to more than one source for guidance can be less useful and confusing. Hence, referring to only one source or a book is important. I believe, this book written by my senior colleagues Mr. Nishant Jain IAS, is one such book. This book guides the aspirants about all crucial dimensions of CSE in a very simple manner. I am sure you will like the way in which the author has explained various complex aspects of CSE. This book is useful for both the beginners and for aspirants who are preparing since last few years. I am sure that the aspirants would immensely benefit from this book.
My best wishes.

—Ansar shaikh
IAS 2016

❍❍❍

"In this book, Nishant drew from his experience of acing the CSE to list down concrete, practical suggestions for the UPSC aspirants. I've always believed that for majority of UPSC aspirants, a major obstacle in clearing CSE is not the lack of study material but abundance of it. Very often aspirants get overwhelmed with deluge of information floating around in the market. Nishant aptly addresses this core issue along with other important dimensions relating to this exam comprehensively so as to make the path easier for an aspirant. I am confident that this book adds tremendous value to every aspirant's UPSC exam preparation. "

—Anudeep Durishetty
IAS, Rank 1, UPSC- 2017

❍❍❍

Preface

Dear friends,

In the 'Ethics' paper of Civil Services Examination, 2014, there was a question : 'What is the definition of Joy'? I wrote, "Joy of Giving or the joy of helping others". In our whole life, we do help others in many ways, and at times, selflessly. You too must have definitely helped someone, and must have derived infinite and unique pleasure from your good deeds.

When the result of Civil Services Examination came out in a grilling afternoon of July, 2015; and when I got an unexpected success, I felt that now I would be able to feel the joy of helping others even more. The beauty of Civil Services is that it provides you not only a platform to do a commendable work in various walks of life, but also a wonderful opportunity to share your rich experiences. Thus, you derive a pleasure from the 'Joy of Giving' by contributing towards the success of others.

A young aspirant can dream of securing the best rank in I.A.S. examination but it is not necessary that the required means and resources are available to them.

At times, they face various hindrances and problems in their path of success i.e. their language or medium of study, their rural and socio-economic background. Sometimes, such circumstances lead to despair, doubts and depression.

Here, the most pertinent question is whether there is any method which can help us in getting out of such circumstances, fill us with positivity and motivation, and fulfill our dream of achieving success. This book is a small effort in this direction. Besides this, it is an honest effort to address all the queries and doubts being raised by the young aspirants from time to time.

Apart from this, there is one more reason behind writing this book. At several occasions, I happened to interact with the young aspirants after my selection in the Civil Services Examination. I could feel their desperation for a complete book, based on the latest syllabus for the overall preparation of the Civil Services Examination. In fact,there are many aspects related with this examination, which they are not aware of. Thus,while preparing for the examination,they may commit some mistakes which can be avoided through a proper guidance.

Besides this, there are hundreds of aspirants who cannot leave their hometown for the preparations. Therefore, a complete book has become a necessity for those living in the remote villages, towns and cities. I can say that this book is the product of my 'realization of responsibility' and 'commitment'.

Another aspect, which makes this book more useful and special, is its adaptability for the young aspirants of Civil Services as well as for those aspirants who are unable to get a positive result in this examination, inspite of repeated efforts. Summarily, it is a comprehensive book consisting of 16 chapters; has the capability of making positive changes in the approach and is beneficial to such aspirants for the preparations of the Civil Services Examination.

This book is dedicated to such aspirants for the overall preparations of the Civil Services Examination conducted by Union Public Service Commission and State PSCs. Every aspirant, preparing for these prestigious examinations dreams of being a topper and there is nothing wrong in it. Somewhere in my heart, I have also dreamt of getting a good rank and fortunately, I could realize my dream.

I long to discuss the important aspects of this examination and wish to share the complete process of its preparations. However, one must keep in mind that to become a topper, or to become a civil servant, is not everything in life. In fact, to lead a meaningful and quality life, staying stress-free and happy, is more important.

The nature of Civil Services Examination conducted by the Union Public Service Commission and the State Public Service Commission is such that one can not succeed in it without having a holistic view, integrated approach, high motivation level, reasonably good personality and a strong expression power. An effort has been made in this book to discuss all the untouched aspects pertaning to the aims and strategies for the preparations of Civil Services Examination. This makes the book more distinct and special. I would feel obliged and successful if this book benefits and boosts up the morale of even one aspirant.

Lastly, I appeal to the aspirants of Civil Services Examination to dream big, achieve something great in life and to work with full zeal towards the goal. I welcome their suggestions also in this regard.

I express my sincere gratitude towards my family, especially my elder brother—Mr. Prashant Jain (Senior Journalist), who is also my friend, philosopher and guide, my respected teachers and seniors as well as my dear friends. I would like to express my deep gratitude towards the senior officers and the noted authors/personalities who motivated me to write this book. I would also like to thank those successful aspirants, who got selected in the past few years, for sharing the untold stories of their struggle with us. Besides, I would like to thank the magazines 'Drishti Current Affairs Today', 'Safalta', 'Yojana' and 'Kadambini' from which I used my published articles/poems in this book, wherever they were deemed to be quoted according to the context.

Once again, I would like to express my gratitude towards all those people who have motivated me directly or indirectly. In the end, I do recall these lines of the poet Robert Frost-

"The woods are lovely, dark and deep,
but I have promises to keep,
and miles to go before I sleep,
and miles to go before I sleep"

—Nishant
nishantjainias.blogspot.in

Contents

1

Why One Should Prepare for Civil Services Examination?

Some people adapt to the mould of time,
but some people transform the frame of time.

In fact, these poetic lines reflect the aim of life to a certain extent. In fact, every aspirant tries to find the purpose of one's life, i.e., to select a good and suitable career according to one's own inclination, talent, interest and ability; to achieve one's ambitions and attain satisfaction through perfection and to find meaning in life as well as earn a respectable living. To develop one's own personality and to do something unique and great, is the inherent desire of every aspirant. Their tendency of dreaming big ultimately takes the aspirants to the zenith of achievement. Dr Kalam aptly says, *"Dream dream dream! Conduct these dreams into thought, then transform them into action"*.

If an aspirant achieves great in life, he/she becomes a role model in one's own field through an expression of creativity and unprecedented performance in the field of literature, music and arts, engineering, medicine, cinema, sports, politics, administration and social service.

The Fundamental Duties of our Constitution states,

"To strive towards excellence in all spheres of individual and collective activity so that the nation constantly rises to higher levels of endeavour and achievement."

The basic idea of this constitutional fundamental duty is that every citizen, irrespective of the field he/she is engaged in, should improve his/her personal as well as social life and achieve success through continuous efforts.

To clear the Civil Services Examination of Union Public Service Commission, or State Public Service Commissions, and become a part of the Indian Civil Services can be a great option for those who are searching for a meaning in their lives. The pertinent question is that why one should choose the Civil Services (I.A.S., I.P.S., I.F.S., I.R.S. etc.), when there are hundreds of other options for finding meaning in one's life and earning a respectable living. Undoubtedly, before starting the preparation for any examination, one should know very well why one wants to be in that particular field.

In my view, there are always some motivational factors for the young aspirants of the Civil Services. Let us have a brief discussion on some of these factors.

For performing well in any field or examination, a strong desire, dedication, devotion and brio are the pre-requisites, as without a certain level of motivation and enthusiasm, the aspirants may abandon their aim or get diverted from the path of success. Thus, a certain level of motivation and positive thinking is mandatory prior to and during the preparation of Civil Services Examination.

I feel that the Civil Services, by following the values of Constitution of India and the Law, provide a huge opportunity to contribute meaningfully and effectively. These Services are known as the 'Steel Frame' of the country, because they contribute to the implementation and regulation of the plans and schemes in the field of agriculture, industry, employment, law and order, railways and posts, information technology, power, science, education, health, land, revenue, culture and welfare of the marginalized class etc. which are directly or indirectly linked to the lives of the common man.

Another important feature of the Civil Services is the diversity of its work. There is hardly any field in a citizen's life where the Civil Services do not contribute to. The civil servants, by using their talent and ability and by performing well in their respective work-field can play an effective role in the building of the society and country.

The feeling of self-satisfaction and the sense of achieving the meaning of our existence are the important motivational factors behind becoming a Civil Servant. Have you ever imagined the level of happiness and satisfaction when you are able to transform the life of a poor and helpless old woman by getting her pension re-released, which has been stopped for quite some time; or when you succeed in bringing about a positive change in the lives of people from the marginalized class, scheduled caste/Scheduled tribe, backward class, minority, differently abled persons, women, children, senior citizens, landless farmers and laborers from the unorganized sector by implementing the Public Welfare Schemes? Following the principles and values of the Constitution of India, we should work towards the implementation of 'Rule of Law' and become an integral part of the campaign to provide a better environment for the upcoming generations. In the twenty-first century, we need to take an inspiration from the passion of our freedom fighters, and contribute towards the developmental process of the country to make it a 'superpower'.

The teachers, doctors, engineers, chartered accountants, architects, advocates, journalists, artists, bankers, managers, businessmen, industrialists, and social-workers etc. play their respective roles in the various areas of life while Civil Servants contribute directly or indirectly towards the policy-making at the medium to higher level, decision-making and implementation at a magnanimous platform. Let's take the instance of Shree Rajesh Patil, an I.A.S Officer of Odisha cadre,, who worked as a child-labur in a small village in Maharashtra, but when he became a Collector, he made the district, under his jurisdiction free from Child Labour.

The Civil Services can be a better medium for working on the lines of the key teachings of Gandhiji. Gandhiji used to say that, "I will give you a talisman. Whenever you are in doubt or when the self becomes too much with you, apply the following test. Recall the face of the poorest and the weakest man (woman) whom you may have seen, and ask yourself, if the step you contemplate is going to be of any use to him (her). Will he (she) gain anything by it. Will it restore him (her) to a control over his (her) own life and destiny?"

Even a single step taken to fulfill the dream of Gandhiji, can give an immense satisfaction and immeasurable pleasure. The Civil Services provide with such opportunities on a daily basis, when we can take a small but definite step towards fulfilling the dream of Gandhiji.

Undoubtedly, the Civil Services are the highly prestigious and respectable career options for any young aspirant, if he/she longs for the prestige and social recognition. In fact, this 24 × 7 job is a service, not merely a job. The preparation of Civil Services can not be done only because of these reasons. If you dream of joining the Indian Administrative Service, and you possess the requisite enthusiasm, dedication and devotion; then you ought to be keen about the incidents happening all over the world, feel the concern and empathy towards your society and country, and put all your efforts to fulfill your dream. A sky full of hopes awaits you. In this context, Nida Fazli a noted Urdu poet has also written:

"We must not try to express our sorrow
in front of some unknown person,
Just try to work towards
making the things right again.
If we are unable to offer prayer in the
mosque because it's far,
Then try to make a weeping kid laugh
and our prayers will be heard".

❑❑

2

How to Develop One's Personality?

Frank Outlaw, the noted Philosopher wrote:

"Watch your thoughts, they become your words,
Watch your words, they become your actions,
Watch your actions, they become your habits,
Watch your habits, they become your character,
Watch your character, it becomes your destiny".

What should the youth from small cities do, so that their chances of succeeding in this prestigious examination might increase? They plan to achieve something in life, aspire for the most prestigious and the toughest examination. What changes or qualitative reforms should these young aspirants incorporate in their personality so that they can reach their goals? On the basis of my limited knowledge and experience, I would try to answer the questions which often come in the mind of these young aspirants.

Civil Services Examination is a complete test of your personality and perspective. In this examination, various aspects of your personality are tested directly or indirectly. Therefore, by making some necessary and effective changes in one's overall personality, an aspirant can increase the possibility of success to an extent.

The following are some relevant points, which are specifically related to the Civil Services Examination; and are helpful in the development of one's personality:

Maintain a Level of Confidence

During the elaborate and tiresome process of preparing for the Civil Services Examination, it often happens that you start doubting about your medium, your optional subject, your ability or even your own capability of clearing this examination. There is nothing wrong in feeling demotivated; but do not get indulged in your doubts to such an extent that you become restless and impatient, and start building a doubtful and negative view of each and every aspect,i.e, 'I cannot get selected' or 'I can never write good answers' etc, as such doubts can become a matter of concern. When I look back, I recall that I always have had a full faith in the examination process, in my medium, in my subject, in my ability, and above all, in my own capability. I feel that such type of faith helps you in performing well in the examination. For example, if any aspirant thinks that, 'my answers will not be evaluated properly', then he/she will not be able to write the answers with 100% presence of mind. This beauty of faith has been expressed in Agyeya's epic Hindi poem 'Asadhya Veena' in the following manner:

"I am not to be credited,
I myself delved deep into infinity,
With the help of Veena I had,
Given myself to infinity,
What you heard is not mine,
It neither belongs to Veena,
That was the extreme of infinity,
The great infinity,
He is highly silent,
Undividable, inanimate, impervious, inexhaustible,
One who is speechless,
Sings within each and every one of us".

Veena-A multistringed chordophone of the Indian subcontinent.

Nurture your Will Power, Ambitions and Brio

We have come across hundreds of examples where the aspirants, after facing serious challenges, have paved their path, and have overcome the challenges by sheer dint of brio and persistence. Maithilisaran Gupta, noted Hindi poet, has written:

"The more hardships a person faces, the more successful one becomes,
The more successful a person becomes, the more name and fame one achieves".

The level of your will power should be your determination to move forward, whatsoever the circumstances may be, and to pave the way on your own. However at the same time, it should be kept in mind that this should not be affected by 'indulgence'. When you move ahead in life with your will power, without caring about the outcome of your deeds, the probability of your success increases manifolds.

One can avoid unnecessary stress and pressure and can ensure excellent performance by doing preparations with such positive attitude. Whether you succeed in the examination or not, your life never stops. You should always keep trying to succeed in life, irrespective of the medium; as 'Success' is a journey, not a destination.

Three Guiding Principles

I have been always guided by the three principles of Indian Philosophy in my journey to achieve success in the Civil Services Examination, as well as in every walk of life. These principles have played a pivotal role in my success.

The first guiding principle is the '**Nishkaam Karmayoga**' from Gita, which prescribes that:

"Karmany evadhikaras te,
ma phaleshu kadachana,
ma karma-phala-hetur-bhur,
ma te sango 'stv akarmani".

(You have a right to perform your prescribed duty but you are not entitled to the fruits of action. Never consider yourself the cause of the results of your activities and never be attached to not doing your duty.)

In a simple language, the principle of 'Nishkaam Karmayoga' (Disinterested or detached Action) means: 'Just do your action, do not wish for its outcome'. Here arises one question in our mind that if we do not have to wish for the outcome of our actions, how we will be motivated to do actions.

According to my understanding of 'Nikshkaam Karmayoga', it does not prohibit you to wish for the outcome, instead it inspires you to do action without getting indulged in it, so that you can achieve the outcome. The 'Nishkaam Karmayoga' has been explained by Dharmaveer Bharati in his lyrical play, 'Andha Yug',in the following manner:

"When any person
Challenges history without being attached to it,
Then that very day the position of stars changes.
Destiny is not predetermined
It changes every moment with the decision
that a person makes".

The positive impact of 'Nishkaam Karmyoga' is visible at every level of the examination. When you prepare for the examination with complete attentiveness, while being unattached to its outcome, where as, getting highly attached in the outcome of the preliminary or the mains examination in which you have just appeared, and wasting the time in guessing its outcome, instead of starting the preparations for the mains examination or for the interview, is a negative approach. By doing so, you stop enjoying the things which you have learnt daily while preparing for The Civil Services Examination. Therefore, in order to remain steady and strong in the preparations of Civil Services Examination, you must incorporate the principle of 'Nishkaam Karmayoga' into your personality with a positive approach.

The second guiding principle is the '**Anekantavad and Syadwad**' (non-absolutism) in the Jain philosophy, which I believe in. The gist of this unique principle is that 'each and every person looks at the truth from a different point of view, but none of the view is either completely right or completely wrong'. Do you remember the example of 'The Elephant and The Seven Blind men'? The seven blind men encounter an elephant on a road-side, and each of them tries to explain the elephant by touching various parts of its body, i.e., one explains it as a broom, while the other explains it as a fan and others so on.

The Anekantavad teaches us that it is wrong to consider one's own view as the right one and term the views of others as the wrong ones. This principle teaches us to respect others' views and show acceptance to them also, asthe acceptance is the key to solve all the problems. A writer has very well said that:–

When we don't accept an undesired event, it becomes *Anger*;

when we accept it, it becomes *Tolerance*.

Wehen we don't accept uncertainty, it becomes *Fear*;

when we accept it, it becomes *Adventure*.

When we don't accept other's bad behaviour towards us, it becomes *Hatred*;

when we accept it, it becomes *Forgiveness*.

When we don't accept other's Success, it becomes *Jealousy*;

when we accept it, it becomes *Inspiration*.

Acceptance is the key to handle the life well.

The principle of Anekantavad helps you at each and every step of your preparation for the Civil Services Examination. It acts like a panacea in the mains examination and interview, e.g.,while writing or answering a question,if we respect the views of others in a balanced way, and refrain from taking an extreme view, it is bound to leave a positive impact. Respecting others' ideas and views, prior to and post the examination, makes the path to success easier in every walk of life.

The third principle is the '**Middle Path**' in Buddha's philosophy, also known as the 'Golden Mean'. In it, Buddha advises to discard both the extremes and adopt the middle path. There is one proverb 'Ati saravatra varjayet' which means 'excess of everything is bad'. Middle path shows us a simple and friendly solution to every kind of disputes or debate.

This path helps in building an integrated approach and balanced viewpoint during the preparations of Civil Services Examination. If the element of tolerance is incorporated in our personality, success comes easily to us in every walk of life, i.e.,using easy and simple language, adhering to the word limit, writing neither very long answer nor very short answer; avoiding perfection and select almost correct answer while answering the objective questions and avoiding radical or extreme view in interview etc. If you want to increase your possibility of success in the Civil Services Examination, you must incorporate these three principles of 'Nishkaam Karmayoga', 'Anekantavad' and 'Madhyam Marg' into your personality.

According to my experience, there are other ways also, apart from these three guiding principles of Indian Philosophy, which can reduce the stress during the preparations of Civil Services Examination, and can make the three phases of this prestigious examination (prelims, mains and interview) a bit easier.

Identify your Strength and Move Ahead

Nature has endowed every human being with certain qualities and abilities as well as certain flaws. It is a proven fact that our weakness and abilities change with the time, and we can overcome the weaknesses and increase our abilities by putting in more efforts. In order to do so, one should know and identify one's own weaknesses and strengths. In other words, it is known as 'Self-Introspection'.

As a matter of fact, it is easy to suggest others to self-introspect, but it is extremely difficult to practice it on your own self. To introspect and analyze oneself is a challenging job, and sometimes, even the highly capable persons fail in it. The factor behind this psychology is that we always tend to like the company of those persons who appreciate us overlooking our shortcomings. Kabir, the great Sufi poet, has recommended to keep the company of even your own critics, as quoted below:

"Keep your critics close to you, let their hut be in your courtyard,
That way you will not need soap and water to cleanse your nature".

Therefore, in the context of preparations of the Civil Services Examination, it is essential to develop an ability of identifying our strengths and weaknesses in our own personality. Especially, if we are able to do this homework at the very beginning of our preparations for the Civil Services Examination, then we can sharpen our qualities and abilities a bit more, and in this way, we can overcome our shortcomings to a great extent.

Maintain Consistency in your Personality

A proverb says,"Winners don't do the different things, they do the things differently". Thus the winners are those who do the things differently and consistently. We know many persons who begin their preparations in an ambitious way, but they don't sustain with the same enthusiasm till the end. Similarily, there are many who lose their patience when they face difficulties in their path or they start making the excuses and blaming the circumstances. Neverthless, there are hundreds of examples of those persons who, due to the element of consistency in their personality, have become successful not only in the Civil Services Examination, but also in other spheres of life.

Now-a-days, there has been a great change in the yardsticks to judge the ability of a person. Earlier, the Intelligence Quotient (IQ) was the basis of judging the ability of a person, later the Emotional Quotient(EQ) was included in it, but lately, the employers have started judging the Pessistence Quotient (PQ) of their future officials/ employees. If any official/employee is assigned a project and his interest and zeal starts fading after a few days, then the probability of his project becoming successful diminishes. Therefore, maintaining the consistent zeal and persistence, the chance of success increases manifold. Harivansh Rai Bachchan, the great poet, has highlighted the quality of persistence in the following words:

"Till the moment you get success, sacrifice your comforts,
Don't leave the battle field and never run away.
Without putting certain efforts, you do not get acclaimed,
And the people who keep on trying, never lose".

Always Keep your Positive Attitude

An aspirant, who is determined to succeed, if he/she always possesses the quality of being positive, then the positive mindset gives an edge over the rest of the aspirants.It is not a cakewalk to maintain the positivity and motivation level during the long and tiresome process of preparations for the Civil Services Examination; but with a sincere effort, this can be achieved. Based on my experience, I can say that the following measures can help in keeping the level of positivity:

(i) Always be happy from within and make others happy. Instead of taking too much stress about studies, it is better start enjoying it.

(ii) Do celebrate all the small happy moments, and never postpone its celebration to tomorrow. I mean, do not say that you will be happy or will celebrate only after achieving your objective. Liveliness should be maintained, and for this, you must not wait for any particular occasion to be happy.

(iii) Sometimes, you may feel motivated after meeting someone, while sometimes, you feel demotivated.

Therefore, always be in the company of people with positive vibes and maintain a safe distance from the people full of negativity. Move forward on your path with loads of positivity, and avoid indulging in meaningless arguments with the negative persons. However, you must welcome openheartedly the healthy criticism and suggestions, meant for your improvement.

(iv) Learn to maintain your relationships. Your family and friends always remain with you during the process of preparation for the examination as well as at every step of life. They motivate you to never lose your confidence and will power.

(v) Develop your interests. Each and every person amongst us can have different interests,i.e., some may like to play, while some like to read; some may like to practise yoga, while some may be interested in watching cinema or listening to music. You must devote at least some time towards your hobbies. It will give you immense pleasure and satisfaction, refresh you as well as maintain your positivity. It will teach you on how to celebrate the small happy moments and how to avoid taking stress on small things.

I, during my Civil Services Examination, wrote the following poem on the 'Positive Thinking'. Its English version is as follows:–

Positive Thinking

"With positive thinking, along with zeal and happiness,
I will win every lost battle; I do believe this in my heart.
Let all the stresses, confusions, anxieties be vanished,
Let there be thousand hindrances in my path,
I will have smile on my face.
Our inner heart must be filled with energy;
that must flow from within,
I will tackle every challenge and conquer the whole world.

Let us take the resolution of creativity with loads of hopes,
destination comes close to committed souls.
Let the wisdom and love be come forth,
and the message should flow; and should give such a message
A new energy should awaken my country till the goal is reached."

Always have a Desire for Learning

The desire for learning is a specific quality in human beings, which makes them not only different from other beings, but also extremely powerful. This very desire of learning motivates them to make new discoveries, move forward and keep making new improvements constantly. The strong desire to learn is always present in a child since the initial stages, and it learns things quickly with the help of imitation. In this manner, the learning process grows to expand the dimensions of our thoughts, and we mature day by day. We continue to learn from our family, friends, teachers, neighbours, surrounding elements, and also from the information provided through the newspapers, magazines, internet and social media.

The preparations for the Civil Services Examination requires a certain level of maturity, which is definitely not related to our physical age. There are aspirants with an open mind, who develop a balanced and broad view at a young age comparatively; while some, though mature in age, they remain stuck in their limited thinking. Therefore, a maturity of ideas and a desire to learn continuously are the essential factors, which lead to success in the Civil Services Examination.

The sea of knowledge is infinite and inexplicable, and we taste only a few drops from it. No doubt, the syllabus for the examination of civil services (Union Public Service Commission and State Public Service Commissions) is very detailed and broad, but the insatiable hunger of the aspirants for a continuous learning makes this multidimensional examination easier, and paves their way for success. Therefore, do not hesitate to learn even from your younger ones, and constantly observe the surroundings and the incidents happening all over the world. In this way, the lifelong learning develops your abilities and helps in achieving success in the Civil Services examination and all walks of life as well.

Develop Aptitude and Attitude

Generally, in order to succeed in any field of life, an attitude and aptitude in that area is essential. Your interest or inclination in a particular field increases the possibility of your success in that field. In this era of specialization, if you want to become a good manager, a teacher or a research scholar, then your respective aptitude for management, teaching or research is tested; but the testing process in the Civil Services Examination is a bit different from those of other competitive examinations. In this examination, the specialization in any specific field is not tested, instead, the basic understanding and views about the various spheres of common life are tested. This examination expects the aspirants to be a generalist, not a specialist.

The Civil Services Examination is different in its nature, as it selects those visionary aspirants who possess the basic understanding of the surroundings, a broad viewpoint and a desire to learn. In order to prepare the selected aspirants for a challenging career,the skills of the selected aspirants are polished through an excellent training. Though the famous proverb says, "Jack of all trades, master of none", but it requires the following modification to suit the need of Civil Services Examination: "Jack of all trades, master of one". We should keep in mind that this examination demands a generalist approach, therefore, an aspirant should mould his/her interests accordingly. Try to keep the following points in mind during the process of developing your attitude and aptitude, while building your personality:

(i) Maintain your awareness of the different dimensions of the incidents and their socio-economic and politico-cultural impact I on the world and society. Update yourself continuously.

(ii) Try to feel the 'Joy of giving'. Make the social concerns as an integral part of your thinking in life, and analyze your contribution towards the marginalized class and the people in need.

(iii) Whenever you feel difficulty in taking the right decisions, or are unable to understand the issue, use your common sense. Though we all possess a common sense, but we fail to use it wisely. During the preparation of Civil Services Examination, or while appearing in the examination, always let your common sense guide you wisely.

In order to build an overall personality, avoid the narrow views and welcome the new ideas with open mind. Learn continuously, and let the best ideas come to us from across the world, as the Rigveda recommends,

"Aa no bhadrah karatvo yantu vishwatah".

(Let noble thoughts come to us from every side)

Therefore, refrain from the narrow mindedness, and adopt a broad and balanced view instead.

There is no Substitute for Hard Work

There is a proverb, **'Practice makes a man perfect'** means that practice enables a person to achieve excellence, as the rope creates a spot on the stone of a well, where it strikes continuously. Therefore, there is no other substitute for practice and hard work. Besides, there is no shortcut to success also; and moving forward continuously, step by step, leads to success.

This proverb is very relevant in the context of the Civil Services Examination. An aspirant can crack this extremely tough examination by the dint of hard work and perseverance. You have to maintain your tendency of doing hard work as you have to work hard and face challenges during your service period too.

Try to Remain Humble in all Situations

While building your personality, during the preparation of the Civil Services Examination, you must develop the quality of remaining humble in all the situations. Humility is such a quality, which makes you, and the people associated with you, happy.

The fact is that the more we learn, the more we realize the truth that we have to learn much more to achieve success. Socrates, the renowned philosopher, said meaningfully, **"The only true wisdom is in knowing you know nothing".** Therefore, remain humble in all the situations and maintain your desire to learn more, while moving forward to achieve success.

Develop your Inherent Skills

Generally, every person is full of abilities. How do we consider one particular person more able than others? As a matter of fact, the yardstick to judge the ability of a person is the skill, which is inherent in the personality of that person.Interestingly, we can develop our inherent skills by devoting ourselves to hard work.

In 'Management Studies', we study that the skills are of the following three types-

(i) Technical skills
(ii) Conceptual skills
(iii) Human skills

If we try to understand these three skills in the context of the Civil Services Examination, then our knowledge, strategy, practice, revision etc. come under the technical skills; our opinion, understanding and analysis of various concepts come under the conceptual skills; and our indomitable spirit, the zeal to learn, aptitude and attitude, as well as the communication skills and the interpersonal skills, come under the human skills.

It is needless to say that all the three sets of skills are required to develop one's overall personality to succeed in the Civil Services examination. Therefore, the aspirants should incorporate these three skills into their personality and keep working on it.

Maintaining Relations

During the preparations of Civil Services examination, it does not always happen that you live your life in a 'straight line.' The moment you start preparing for this examination, you are bound to face the ups and downs. In such a situation, you need the support of your parents, siblings and close friends.

For staying stress-free and happy, it is necessary to maintain these relations, not only during the preparations of examination, but also for your whole life.

❑❑

3 Holistic Preparation: Understanding the New Pattern

Preparation for Civil Services examination is a holistic and comprehensive process in itself. It is quite necessary to understand the fact that the toppers do not make any extraordinary preparation; they study the same books and study materials. Their preparations are almost the same as those of the other aspirants. Then, what are the factors which help them in achieving the desired success? In the previous chapter, we discussed the manner in which an aspirant should develop one's personality. In this chapter, we will understand the practical aspects of the overall preparations for the civil services examination. First of all, let us try to understand the scheme of exam and the latest pattern of this examination.

Scheme of Civil Services Examination

The highly prestigious Civil Services Examination is conducted every year by the Union Public Service Commission to select the deserving candidates for the various All India Services, Central Services (Group-A and Group-B) of Government of India.

The examination is conducted in three phases: Preliminary, Mains and Interview.

In the Preliminary examination, two papers are to be attempted in a day, consisting of Multiple Choice Questions. It is a kind of screening examination, because its marks are not added in the final merit. The success in the preliminary examination leads to the mains exam.

The Mains examination, is the most important phase of the Civil Services Examination. Your success depends mainly on this phase. It consists nine written papers, which are conducted usually over a span of one week.

The candidates, selected in the Mains examination, are called for an Interview (Personality Test) at the Commission's office in Delhi. Generally against the total vacancy, nearly two and a half or three times of the vacancies are called for the interview.

Generally, the preliminary examination is conducted in May-June, the mains examinationin October-November, and the interview in the beginning of next year, i.e., in February-March. The Foundation Course,the first phase of the training of the finally selected candidates,begins in August-September at the Lal Bahadur Shastri National Academy of Administration in Mussoorie.

The basic facts of the Civil Services Examination:

Services

This prestigious examination is conducted to select the deserving candidates for the following All India Services and Central Services at the all India level:

- Indian Administrative Service (IAS)
- Indian Foreign Service (IFS)
- Indian Police Service (IPS)
- Indian Post &Telegraph Accounts and Finance Service
- Indian Audit and Accounts Service (IAAS)
- Indian Revenue Service(Income Tax) (IRS-IT)
- Indian Revenue Service (Customs & Central Excise) (IRS-C & CE)
- Indian Ordinance Factory Service (IOFS)
- Indian Civil Accounts Service (ICAS)
- Indian Defense Accounts Service (IDAS)
- Indian Railway Accounts Service (IRAS)
- Indian Railway Traffic Service (IRTS)

- Indian Railway Personnel Service (IRPS)
- Indian Postal Service (IPoS)
- Indian Defence Estates Service (IDES)
- Indian Information Service (IIS)
- Indian Trade Service (ITS)
- Indian Corporate Law Service (ICLS)
- Assistant Security Commissioner in Railway Protection Force (RPF)
- Armed Force Headquarters Civil Serives Group 'B' (AFHQ)
- Delhi, Andaman-Nicobar Islands, Lakshadweep, Daman-Diu, Dadar and Nagar Haveli Civil Service Group-B (DANICS)
- Delhi, Andaman and Nicobar Islands, Lakshadweep, Daman and Diu, Dadar and Nagar Haveli Police Service (Group-B) (DANIPS)
- Pondicherry Civil Service (Group-B)
- Pondicherry Police Service (Group-B)

The candidates, who succeed in the preliminary examination, have to fill up their preferences of the services in a form, sent by the Commission. The preferences for the State Cadres for I.A.S and I.P.S are also to be filled up in the same form.

Division of Marks in the Three Phases of Examination

Preliminary Examination

- Paper-I: General Studies, consisting 100 questions, carries 200 marks.
- Paper-II: General Studies (C-SAT), consisting 80 questions, carries 200 marks
- Both the papers have the multiple choice questions. Since the Preliminary examination is a kind of screening examination, so in both the papers, for each wrong answer, one-third of the total marks allotted to the question are deducted.

The candidates who pass it, get an opportunity to appear in the mains examination.

Mains Examination

This exam comprises of nine papers. Out of these nine papers, two papers are the qualifying papers, i.e., the English and any one of the Indian languages, to be chosen from the 22 languages listed in the Eighth Schedule of the Constitution of India. Each qualifying paper carries 300 marks; and the marks obtained in these two papers are not added in the final merit. The remaining seven papers in the mains examination, which are included in the merit, are as following:

1. Essay
2. General Studies-I
   (Indian Heritage and Culture, History and Geography of the world and Society)
3. General Studies-II
   (Governance, Constitution, Polity, Social Justice and International Relations)
4. General Studies-III
   (Technology, Economic Development, Bio-diversity, Environment, Security and Disaster Management)
5. General Studies-IV
   (Ethics, Integrity and Aptitude)
6. Optional subject: Paper one
7. Optional subject: Paper two

Each of these seven papers carries 250 marks. In this way, total marks allotted to the mains examination are - 1750.

Personality Test/Interview

The candidates, who are declared successful in the Mains examination, are called for the final phase, i.e., Interview, at the Commission's office in Delhi. The total marks allotted to the Interview is 275. In this way, the total marks allotted for the final merit is 2025 (1750 marks for Mains examination and 275 marks for Interview).

Optional Subjects for the Mains (Written) Examination

The following optional subjects are offered for the Mains examination:

- Agriculture
- Animal Husbandry and Veterinary Science
- Anthropology
- Botany
- Chemistry
- Civil Engineering
- Commerce and Accountancy
- Economics
- Electrical Engineering
- Geography
- Geology
- History
- Law
- Management
- Mathematics
- Mechanical Engineering
- Medical Science
- Philosophy
- Physics
- Political Science and International Relations
- Psychology
- Public Administration
- Sociology
- Statistics
- Zoology
- Literature of any one of the Indian languages from the 22 languages mentioned in the Eighth Schedule of the Constitution of India and English.

One optional subject is to be selected from the above given list. The optional subject consists of two papers of

250 marks each. I have devoted a separate chapter in this book on the selection of optional subject.

Understanding the New Pattern

There have been major changes in the Civil Services Examination, conducted by the Union Public Service Commission. The first major change was made in the year 2011, when the commission changed the pattern of the preliminary exam and introduced the General Studies Paper-II (C-SAT), and both the General studies and C-SAT were of 200 marks each. Till the year 2014, marks of both the papers were added equally in the preliminary examination. Afterwards, one more change was introduced in 2015 in the preliminary examination. It was decided that from now onwards, the marks of Paper-II, i.e. C-SAT will not be added, and this paper will be treated as a qualifying paper only. Since then, only the marks of Paper-I, i.e., General Studies (G.S.), are being added in the preliminary examination.Therefore, the path to success in the civil services examination goes through the General Studies.

The second major change was made in the year 2013 in the mains examination. Earlier, it has consisted of two optional subjects, now there is only one;earlier, the General Studies has consisted of two papers, now there are four.The new paper of 'Ethics' was introduced in the form of Paper-IV of the General Studies.

In this manner, the marks, scored in these seven papers in the mains examination, are added in the final merit; and the two papers (Compulsory languages) are qualifying in nature. The seven papers, are of 250 marks each; and the interview carries 275 marks, which totals to 2025 marks.

The new pattern seems to be more logical, as the weightage of the papers of Essay and General Studies has been increased considerably. The Optional Subject has been reduced to just one optional subject. if we analyze the marks secured by the toppers in recent years, we will find that the path of becoming a topper in the civil services examination goes through the papers of Essay and General Studies - Paper-IV, i.e., Ethics. We will discuss this topic in the chapter, devoted to the Mains examination.

How to Start Preparations?

The aspirants, dreaming to be selected in the Civil Services, are often confused, as to when and how to start their preparations for this examination. My suggestion to them is to start a dedicated preparation for this examination just after their graduation. However, there are examples of the aspirants, who had started their preparation after the post-graduation, got selected. If you are dreaming of success in the civil services examination with good marks, it is better to start your preparations just after completing your graduation.

However, if some aspirant starts planning for the civil services after the 12th class itself, then I suggest him/her to focus on his/her graduation. Simultanously, he/she should start developing an interest and orientation towards the civil services examination.

Your graduation can be treated as a starting point for preparation of this exam. This not only provides you with an option of a prestigious career, but also helps you at every stage of this examination. For example, during the interview, you will not face any difficulty in answering the questions, asked from your own subject of graduation.

The aspirants, who have already begun their preparations, must read the newspapers and monthly magazines regularly. They must go through the previous years' exam- papers. They should read the NCERT books of Class IX to XII as well. Such an orientation will familiarize them with the preparation process of this examination. As already said,there is no issue if you have not been oriented towards this examination earlier, and you want to start your preparation after completing the graduation/ post-graduation or research.

Many aspirants are keen to know about how much time is sufficient for doing the preparations of this examination. Though, the time after completing your graduation/post-graduation or research is sufficient for the preparations of this examination,but still in my view, a dedicated one year or a year and a half is required for preparing thoroughly for this examination. Apart from this, the three phases of the examination, i.e., Prelims, Mains and Interview, continue for about eight to nine months. Therefore, I will prescribe you to maintain your patience and motivation throughout the whole process.

How to Choose Medium of Examination?

Many aspirants struggle to choose one Indian language as their medium for the examination.

Of course, you have the option of choosing any one Indian language out of 22 languages, including English as your medium for the Civil Services examination; but then you will have to write all the papers of the Mains examination (excluding qualifying language) in the selected language only. It is not possible that you write the General Studies paper in English and the optional subject paper in Hindi or Tamil.

As far as the question of selecting the medium of examination is concerned, I suggest you to select only that language as your medium, in which you have full command and you can express yourself in a better way. The aspirants, who have studied in only one language medium from the primary classes to graduation, do not get confused while selecting the language medium. For example, I studied in the Hindi medium from the primary classes to the higher classes, therefore, I was very clear about my medium of language for the Civil services examination.I knew that though my English is reasonably good, but my Hindi is much better than English in terms of expressing myself. Therefore, I selected the Hindi as my medium for the civil services examination. There are some aspirants who study in Hindi or vernacular language medium till Class XII, but they do their graduation and post-graduation in English medium. In such a situation, the confusion of selecting the appropriate medium arises the most. I advise them that they should go through the previous years' papers before selecting the medium; and then should try to assess their command over the language in which they are able to comprehend the paper well, and are able to express themselves better. No doubt, the position of English medium is comparatively better in terms of the study materials and guidance, but now-a-days, good and authentic books and guidance are available in Hindi and some other Indian languages.

In brief, one should keep the following points in mind,priority-wise, before selecting any language as the medium for the Civil Services Examination:

1. Your spontaneity and ability to express in that language.
2. The authentic study materials available in that language.
3. The guidance available in that language.
4. The prevalence of that language in the Civil Services examination.

As far as the medium for the interview is concerned, there is a freedom to give interview in a language, other than the medium, in which you have written the Mains examination. There are aspirants who write their Mains examination in English, but appear in the interview with their own language.

Coaching Classes: Myth and Reality

Though it is not essential to join a coaching for success in the examination, but in order to perform well in the examination, proper guidance is quite important for the aspirants. In such a situation, good teachers, seniors, or experts prove to be very helpful. The practice of writing answers can be done in the coaching class and the experts can review your preparations from time to time. Sometimes, the friends who are serious about their preparations, can assist you in the preparation through group discussion.

In this regard, I would advise you that it is not a wise decision to join a coaching institution blindly by imitating someone, or rely on the unauthentic and low grade study materials, and get too much influenced by the advertisements.

If you want to join a coaching, since you require it, you should keep your eyes and ears open while attending the classes, and follow the authentic books, magazines and websites also (A detailed description has been given in the chapter 'Knowing what to study and what not). Here, understand one thing that you need not read a topic from multiple sources. If you have studied a topic from one authentic source, then you need not study the same topic from other sources.

If your optional subject is not from your educational background, and it is new to you, then it is better to take guidance for it from some expert or coaching class.

Right Planning Approach: A Key to Success

Generally, when we begin the overall preparations for the Civil Services Examination, a confusion arises regarding a proper division of time to utilize it the maximum; and most importantly, how to divide the time among the three phases of the examination, the prelims, mains and interview. Sometimes, we are also confused about how much time should we devote on various papers and the whole process.

As such, it is better to do the right planning to avoid the uninvited confusion. Always remember the following paradigm during your preparations for the civil services examination:

1. Plan (How to study),
2. Learn (What to study),
3. Share (Knowledge),
4. Achieve (Our goal)

Here, one thing is worth noting that one must always keep a sufficient scope for the changes and improvement in one's planning for the examination. One must not keep sticking to the previous plan, even after getting the new inputs or information. I advise you to begin your overall preparations for the preliminary and mains examination simultaneously. It is essential that you should select your optional subject in the beginning of your preparations itself, and start preparing for it. Your preparations of the optional subject should complete by December-January. For about three months, before the preliminary examination, you should focus only on this phase. After appearing in the examination, you should not wait for its result. You must start preparing for the mains examination. It is my suggestion that you should not worry about the interview in the beginning of your preparations,as the time, which you get after appearing in the mains examination, is sufficient for prepartion for the interview.

Sometimes, this planning process has a major drawback.,as some aspirants, though excellent in planning, but they are poor in its implementation; they get so much involved in planning that they keep planning for a long time. There is a saying, *"Well done is better than well said"*. Therefore, you should not do a detailed planning in the beginning, instead you should prepare a general plan and pay your full attention to your studies. It is a proven fact that all of us have some weak as well as strong traits in our personality,but we should be aware of them. The statement,*"It is not a bad thing to possess weakness, but not identifying them is wrong"*, is very relevant in this context.

SWOT Analysis for Self-Evaluation

SWOT means:

- S—Strengths,
- W—Weakness,
- O—Opportunities,
- T—Threats.

It is important to evaluate yourself in the beginning and during your preparations through the SWOT analysis. However, you can take the help of the members of your family, teachers and friends for this purpose, without any hesitation.

When we understand our strengths and weaknesses, we are able to make our strong aspects stronger, and can reduce the negative effects of our weak aspects. In addition, we can be aware of the opportunities and challenges, which we come across in the process of preparation for the examination, and thus can avoid the same mistakes in future.

Risk Analysis

Generally in Economics, when we start any new project, we do the 'Cost-benefit analysis' and 'Risk-analysis' to understand the prospective profit and loss, to know the risk involved, and to take the decision accordingly.

Though, it is not directly related to the Civil Services Examination, but still, I would suggest you to understand the prospective profit and loss and the risk involved. For example, if you are devoting your full time for the Civil Services Examination, then, just think that had you not been involved in the preparations, you would have been involved in some other productive or economic activity, like,doing a job, running a business or agricultural activities etc.

Always keep in mind, that you should not be lenient towards your preparations at any cost; and you should not overthink and get stressed as well. Once you have decided to prepare for the civil services, you should go ahead with it with full dedication.

Taking risk is another important factor to achieve success. You must have heard the proverb, 'No risk, no gain'. There is no doubt in the fact that if we wish to achieve something big in life, we have to take big risks. But there is one more proverb, "*Don't put all the eggs in one basket*',which means that you should not put yourself at a big risk. Try to reduce the risk-factor. Therefore, to reduce the risk-factor to a certain extent, try to think of some other career option or attain a level of employability.

What to Learn from Previous Years' Papers?

I would like to specially emphasize that you must frequently go through and analyze the papers of previous years, during the preparations. You can learn many things by studying and analyzing the previous year papers (both prelims and mains) on a frequent intervals. It will help you to comprehend the important aspects. At the same time, you will also understand the level of examination more clearly. My experience says that you should go through the papers of at least previous five years. However, going through the very old papers do not benefit you much.

How Many Hours Should we Study?

The aspirants often ask this question to the toppers of the civil services examination. I would like to clarify that there is no fixed formula for the number of hours; therefore, one should not get involved into the issue of number of hours. It would be better to fix small targets and achieve them one by one. Small targets should be fixed like, 'Today I have to study this much', instead of 'Today I have to study for so and so hours'; and you will find that it is more beneficial. The most important thing is that you should focus more on deciding, 'what to study', rather than on 'how long to study'.

Time Management is the Key

It is said that the intelligent person is the one who does the maximum utilization of the available time.

So, you must learn the art of time management. You should analyze how one person, while completing all the necessary tasks, still manages to devote some time for his/her interests, where as another person, who is continuously busy, but still is unable to complete his/her tasks or duties.

There are many such aspirants, who remain busy for the most of the time but their output is comparatively less. Due to their disorganized routine, they are unable to achieve even their small targets.

Hence, my suggestion is that you should prepare a general routine, and try to follow it as far as possible. For example, try to follow the routine of sleeping and waking up, walking and exercising, reading the newspaper and doing the writing practice. Often, it happens that we do prepare a very good routine, but we fail to implement it. Another thing is that, generally, most of us fail to follow the routine properly and we start taking stress. As none of us is perfect, so instead of worrying, move forward without taking any stress of the earlier flaws.

If you are doing the preparations along with the job, in my view, there are two ways of doing the preparations in this situation. The first type is that you start preparing after joining your job. The second type is that first you devote one or one and a half year for the preparations; and once you complete it,you can join a part-time or full-time job. There is no problem in the second type of doing preparations. If you have already covered the whole syllabus once, then you can easily do the revision along with your job and can prepare the new current affairs. Doing preparations along with a job is a challenging task, but not an impossible task. One very positive aspect of doing a job, along with the preparations, is that it increases your confidence and experience, and it helps you doing the preparations without stress.

How to Make Notes?

Making the study- notes is an important strategy, which the successful aspirants usually follow. It proves to be very beneficial. Some of the benefits of making the study-notes are: - firstly, it helps completing the syllabus and also revising it; second, it helps retaining the content written in your own style from various sources and it also helps developing the writing skills.

Every aspirant has his/her own way of making the study- notes,e.g., some make the notes in a separate notebook from their own study materials, while some only highlight or underline the important points in the book itself; some make full notes of the important topics,and only highlight or underline the book for the less important topics. In my view, you can choose one of the two above methods, or you can follow both the methods at the same time.

However, while making the study-notes, keep some important points in your mind,i.e., never underline or highlight on the pages so much that it becomes difficult for you to find the important portion; secondly, make notes in brief, keeping in mind that you are making your study-notes with the objective to make your preparations and revision easy, not to write a new book.

I have one more suggestion regarding the making of study-notes, make a diary and write down the name of study materials and books, from which you have studied the various topics. This small but useful habit of noting down the sources will help you in doing a quick revision during the time of examination.

Prior to the examination, every aspirant feels the stress; and it is quite natural. Therefore, avoid the stress before the examination, so that it can not affect your performance adversely. To avoid the stress just before the examination, there is one useful strategy: you decide the things to study and the topics to revise in advance.

Smart Study Tips

There are aspirants, who study all the time, but they lag behind when the time of giving an output or performing in the exam comes. In contrast, there are such aspirants, who study less, but they study in a smart and organized manner and become successful. Thus, because of doing a 'smart study' they perform very well.

I am not advising to study less. Here, I mean to say that, your output should be according to your inputs and efforts, which you are giving to your studies. The way to perform well in the examination has already been discussed in this chapter. Here, we will discuss how to do a smart study and improve your way of studying.

According to my experience, here are some tips for smart study:-

- Enjoy your studies. The overall process of preparations for the Civil Services Examination is broad and complete in itself. During the preparations, you get acquainted with the various dimensions of social, cultural, economic, political, philosophical, scientific and technical aspects of the society and the world.Enjoy whatever new things you learn during this preparation process. It will not only give you the pleasure and satisfaction, but also it will keep you free from the stress.
- *Study less, comprehend well.* It means that whatever you study, you should fully comprehend it, before moving ahead. It is also known as contemplation.
- Select few but good books. The study materials for preparing the civil services examination are available in abundance. I would suggest that select fewer books, but the good ones.There is a saying, 'It is better to read one book ten times, than to read ten books one time'.
- Take a break. Generally, a person cannot study continuously for long hours. Therefore, take a break, after studying for one hour. During the break, you can listen to the soft music while walking. It is necessary to take some small breaks during your studies, so that it does not become boring.
- Do not show off. It does not mean that you should hide your skills from the people.It means you should not blow your own trumpet, let your success speak aloud instead.

- Have Group Discussions. A group-discussion not only helps in memorizing the things for a long time, but it also helps in developing more new ideas. Therefore, have the group-discussions with your friends.
- Cover the maximum syllabus. The selective reading does not help much now-a-days. So, you should cover the syllabus in such a way that you should be able to write five to seven points on the given topics, even if you do not have full knowledge of them. Now-a-days, writing long answers is not much required.
- Highlight and revise the important points. After the first reading, try to highlight the important points and revise them. Keep revising them on a regular basis. Your study will become easier by doing so.

How to do Revision?

After knowing 'how to study' and 'how to prepare notes', it becomes necessary to know- 'how to revise', so that we can reproduce the things, which we have read and learnt during our preparations. This learning will be reflected through our good score in the mark sheet.

Study daily according to your planning for the overall exam preparations. You should do the revision regularly, and never leave your study for tomorrow.

Set small targets during your studies, and keep on doing a full revision of it. If you have joined any test series, you can revise the syllabus naturally during your studies for the test. Always remember, you should focus on revision only just before examinations.

Following Integrated and Inter-disciplinary Approach for the Overall Preparations

It is the age of an integrated and inter-disciplinary studies and a comprehensive approach. In this scenario, the Civil

Services Examination has become more dynamic. So while doing preparations, if you constrain yourself and do not extend your thinking process, it will prove to be an impediment.

In general, everything in our lives is interconnected. Similarly, the syllabus and the new pattern of the civil services examination are also interconnected and interrelated,e.g., if the economy is in peril, its effect can be seen on the political scenario and on the societal and international relations. In the same manner, every section of the General Studies is interconnected, directly or indirectly. We need to identify the impact of economy and politics at the national and the international levels; and try to analyze them in relation to one another.

For this, you should possess a balanced and a broad viewpoint. Refrain from any extreme view. Always try to welcome and respect the views of others. This positive approach will help you in developing a broad viewpoint.

Remain Stress-free During Preparations

Although, one is bound to be stressed while preparing for the Civil Services Examination, Some times during the preparations, you get stressed and become unhappy. Though, getting stressed or tensed is a natural phenomenon but it is not advisable to remain in stress for a long time. In such circumstances, give time to your interests and likings, as they will help you in releasing the stress. If you love watching movies, listening to music, travelling or playing, then definitely include your hobby in your routine. If you are unable to do it daily, then do it on a weekly basis,e.g., write a diary, as it is a good hobby.It releases the stress and helps in developing the writing skills. Besides this, do celebrate the small happy moments. Never postpone the celebration of today's happy moments for tomorrow.

You must have met some aspirants, who are always in tension and stress because of their unknown fears. They become habitual of this tendency, though everything is going on as per the plans. Due to this tendency,they stop caring of their physical and mental health; and they stop enjoying their interests and happiness.

Such a negative thinking slowly starts affecting you physically and mentally, and also deprives you of the happy moments of life. In my view, taking a continuous stress is harmful from the point of view of the examination as well as for your future life.

Out of various important ways to remain stress-free while doing preparations, there is an option,i.e., you may think of an career option, as the employability helps in reducing the stress to a certain extent. Not having another career option and focusing on only one career can be the reason for stress. There is no guarantee that one will definitely succeed in the Civil Services Examination, as this examination is full of uncertainty.

You must have heard a proverb,'*Shoot for the moon, even if you miss, you'll land among the stars*'. Therefore, one failure in your life can not define you. You will find numerous opportunities still lying on your path. Never think that the door to success is closed for you. I have discussed this aspect in detail in the chapter 'Civil Services Examination versus Other Career Options'.

In the concusion, I would advise you that never ignore your physical and mental health. Be simple, busy, healthy and joyful, like the hero of the bollywood film, 'Manjhi-The Mountainman', in which Dashrath Manjhi always hums the mantra of "Shandaar-Zabardast- Zindabad". The tendency of setting your friends and family aside, and living alone, will not help you; it will increase your stress and depression instead. If you continuously feel depressed, do not hesitate consulting a counselor or clinical psychologist.

Strive for Continuous Improvement, instead of Perfection

Considering the toppers as the perfect ones, some aspirants tend to imitate them blindly. They try to become perfect like them. The desire to become perfect may take a toll on you. Remember, no one is perfect, as this proverb says:

"There is no perfect way,
There are many good ways".

My suggestion is that do get inspired from them, but do not imitate them blindly. While preparing for the examination,do everything in the best possible way,e.g., if your study materials, coaching, test series are of the best quality, and you are preparing your study-notes, doing your revision, and following your routine in a planned and organized manner, you will definitely get success in the civil services examination.

We must understand that there is hardly any difference between a topper and an aspirant. Most of the toppers, after getting the success, have admitted that they themselves have not had any idea of achieving such an outstanding success. Therefore if an aspirant is intelligent, hard working, and vigorous, he/shecan definitely become a topper in the civil services examination.

Jack of all Trades, Master of One

Apart from the general knowledge and other things,the aptitude of the aspirants is also tested in the Civil Services Examination. In this examination, you are not supposed to be a specialist of any particular subject, you are supposed to be a generalist instead. This prestigious examination is very different from the other examinations. To be successful in it, an aspirant needs to develop a general understanding of the various subjects, like history and culture, science and technology, society, polity, economy, ethics, geography, environment and ecosystem, security and international relations etc.

I have added the phrase 'master of one' in the proverb, because for clearing the mains paper in the Civil Services Examination, an aspirant needs to study adequately and develop a good understanding of the optional subject, apart from the General Studies, essay and compulsory language.

There is no Shortcut to Success

An author has rightly said, "Get included yourself in the list of the aspirants who work hard, as such aspirants are fewer in number, hence the chance of your success becomes manifold". It is true that there is no substitute for the hard work and perseverance and also no shortcut or fixed formula of success. Some aspirants, if they are unable to do the hard work, they start blaming the circumstances. Remember, even if we do not have enough resources, we should not blame the circumstances or get demotivated.

You are a youngster full of positive energy. You are supposed to play a big role in the building of a strong and competent society and nation. R. W. Emerson, the English poet, has also written in his poem, 'A nation's strength:-

"Brave men, who work while others sleep,
Who dare while others fly.
They build a nation's pillars deep,
And lift them to the sky".

Writing Practice cannot be Avoided

It is essential to write and discuss the issues during the process of your study. I have seen some aspirants, who can study and write very well, but they refrain from writing. Therefore, I would suggest you to write, write and write, if you wish to improve your writing skills.

Just gather courage for once, and start your writing practice. Though, to start a new task appears to be difficult, but you will find that your confidence in writing the answers has increased after starting your writing practice. Confidence is the most important thing for writing the answers,and you gain confidence only after continuing your writing practice. Gradually, you will stop committing mistakes, and by the time you appear in the mains examination, the quality of your answers will improve to a great extent.

For the aspirants, there is a mantra to improve their writing skills. Besides, doing the writing practice for attempting the answers of General Studies, practice writing at least one essay and two case studies every week, that too on the plain paper without lines, as in the Civil Services examination, you will be required to write the answers on the plain sheets without lines. If,you practisethis every week during your preparations, you will be able to write the Mains exam with full confidence. A detailed information on this topic is given in the chapter titled, 'Writing Skill: The Basis of Success'.

Learn to Say 'No'

Try to say 'no' to the unimportant things and tasks. Define your priorities and never ignore them. During the preparations, we often say 'yes' to do the tasks, asked by our friends and acquaintances. While trying to make others happy, we often ignore our own priorities. I am not preventing you from maintaining your relations with your friends and acquaintances, but it does not mean that you appease others at the cost of your own studies.

Avoid Confusion

Harivansh Rai Bachchan, the Hindi poet, has written the following lines in his poetic book, 'Madhushala':

"Seeking wine, the drinker leaves home for the tavern,
Perplexed, he asks "which path will take me there?
People show him different ways, but this is what I have to say,
Pick a path and keep walking. You will find the tavern".

No doubt, we should respect the ideas of others, but it is not worthwhile to take the advice from everyone and get confused by listening to the contradictory ideas. It happens during the preparations that you get confused on some matters, but you should not maintain the state of uncertainty and confusion continuously, as it can be detrimental. Instead of remaining confused on those matters, take advice from your trustworthy teachers, friends or experienced senior mates and your family members.

Reading Habit Improves you a Lot

If I ask you, "what you are studying these days", your answer will be: general Studies and Optional subject". At this point, I mean to ask, "whether you study some other books or magazines also, apart from the text-books prescribed in your syllabus".

I would suggest you to spare some time in reading some books or magazines of general interest and convert your answer into 'Yes'.

These books/magazines may not be directly relevant to your preparation, but indirectly, these books do widen the horizon of your thinking; increase your knowledge and experience; entertain you; and improve your writing skills by increasing your word-power,e.g. 'Reader's Digest' the literature of well-known authors; or the fiction and non-fiction books published by the National Book Trust Publications Division and Sahitya Akademi. In this way, your 'General Reading Habit' will pay you in the long run.

You can develop this habit by reading the books and magazines, as well as using the social media. If social media is used with care and in a balanced manner, it can prove to be very helpful. I myself have experienced that the social media has helped me to some extent.

Develop a Certain Level of Maturity

When I talk about the 'maturity', it means the development of qualities, like a balanced viewpoint, an integrated approach, a good reading and writing habit, which develop gradually with the passage of time. An aspirant, who always does serious talks, or shows off his/her knowledge/ experience cannot be termed as a mature person. A person, who has a balanced viewpoint and an integrated approach, is generally considered to be a matured person.

The prestigious Civil Services Examination expects a certain level of maturity from the aspirants. This maturity, not necessarily, comes with the age only. One can be mature at a very young age, where as the others may not be mature despite of being older in age.

You can develop your maturity by developing the good habits. You must inculcate the new good habits, and leave the old habits gradually,e.g., develop the habit of writing, besides reading. You can enhance your maturity by avoiding the extreme viewpoint, and having an integrated approach in your life.

It is a fact that, behind the success of every successful person, there is an endless struggle. It is the struggle that makes him/her more mature with each passing day.

Maintain Relations

Always remember that the knowledge increases by sharing it with others. The 'Tatvartha Sutra' of the Jain philosophy says, "parasparograho jeeawanaam". It means that the living beings get benefitted by helping one another. Therefore, my advice is that help others and take help from others, when needed. Do share the information and ideas among one another. The new things, learnt by you, must be shared within your friend circle, as your learning gets consolidated by telling it to others. Help your friends by advising them not to commit the same mistakes, which you have committed during your preparations.

Your preparation becomes easier, if you are in the company of good guides, teachers and friends. Apart from your family, your friends, classmates and roommates play an important role in continuously maintaining your morale during the preparations. Just try to avoid the negative people, as they can confuse or demoralise you.

Remember, an aspirant's success is never an individual's success, as every person in his/her life has cooperated and contributed in this success directly or indirectly.

Strategy in the Examination Hall

The examiner judges your knowledge and understanding on the basis of your answer sheet. Therefore, the strategy to be followed in the examination hall is quite important. I have always believed, that the level of your performance in the exam hall should match the level of your whole preparation. Hence just before and during the examination, you must keep the following points in mind:–

- Do not take stress of your studies on the day before the examination day. Take light and digestive food and have a sound sleep.
- As per your examination schedule, streamline your sleeping and waking timings in advance, so that you may feel fresh on the day of examination.
- After getting the paper, try to have a quick overview of the whole paper. Fix the time, which you want to devote in answering a question, and try to follow it.
- Try to answer all the questions, asked in the question paper. If you do not get enough time in the end, at least try to write the outlines of your answer, or write only the main points of such questions.
- Presentation is very important. Therefore, do write in a neat and clean manner and in a legible handwriting. Highlight the main points without any hesitation. Although you may not get enough time to use the pen of different colors in the exam, but, you can use a black pen with the blue pen.
- A Questions-Cum-Answer Booklet is being used in the examination, these days, in which you are expected to write the answers in the defined space, given along with each question. In such a situation, try to write the answer in a sequence, i.e., write answers from the beginning till the end. Earlier, when a separate answer sheet used to be provided, we used to write the answers of those questions first, which we knew very well; but this old way has become obsolete now.

- Follow the word-limit strictly. Never count the words in the exam hall. Practice it in advance, and form an idea of the number of words you write on a single page. Based on this practice, define the length and time to be taken for writing your answers. Besides, you should never panic about the gap coming between the word-limits, e.g., If in a paper, you are asked to write the answer in 200 words, and you have written it in 170 words; or in the essay paper, if you miss the word-limit or write 50-100 words more than the prescribed limit, then it is not a big issue.
- In the examination hall, make the maximum utilization of the three hours, provided to you. Do not panic during these hours. Try to maintain your energy level, think that you will never get these three hours in your life again, and write your paper with full zeal and enthusiasm.

❑❑

4

Knowing What to Study and What Not

The aspirants,dedicated towards the preparations of the Civil Services examination, are troubled by certain questions, like 'what to study and what not, in which manner one should study, whether the way of studying for the civil services examination should be similar or different from that of the other competitive exams, which books and magazines should be included in the study materials, and which materials should be ignored etc'. Sometimes, they become apprehensive too, that if they ignore some materials and the others may study it, they may lag behind in the race.

During my preparations,the same questions had troubled me also. I feel that it is quite difficult to make a list of the widely acceptable and accurate books for the preparation of country's most prestigious examination. The nature of the Civil Services Examination is dynamic and unpredictable. However, keeping in mind its new pattern, I have tried to prepare a list of good and authentic study materials to provide an overview of the examination.

List of Books and Sources

On the basis of my understanding, studies and experience, I have prepared a list of books and sources of other study materials. It must be kept in mind, that this list is indicative, and it is not necessary at all to study or go through each and every source mentioned in this list. This list is not ultimate, so it can be expanded or shortened as per the convenience and level of the aspirants.

Books

History: NCERT books from Class 6 to 12; Spectrum's 'A Brief History of Modern India' and; Bipin Chandra's 'Indian Freedom Struggle of Independence' and 'India after Independence', RC Guha's 'India After Gandhi'.

Geography: NCERT books from Class 6 to 12; Books written by Majid Hussain and G.C. Leong, Orient Longman Atlas, Majid Hussain's World Geography.

Polity: M. Laxmikanth's 'Indian Polity' and; M. Laxmikanth's 'Indian Governance', 2nd ARC Report.

Economy: NCERT books from Class 9 to 12; Ramesh Singh's 'Indian Economy'; 'Economic Survey' and 'Budget' published by the Government of India and; Video lectures of Mrunal.

Environment: NCERT books

Science and Technology: Science & Technology–TMH or Spectrum. The Current Affairs related to development in the areas of science and Technology.

Indian Culture: Nitin Singhania's Book and; History of Indian Art, NCERT book of Fine Arts.

Internal Security: Ashok Kumar and Vipul,Published by Tata McGraw Hill.

International Relations: Ministry of Foreign Affairs website: www.mea.gov.in, 'Foreign Policy of India' by VN Khanna.

Indian Society: Ram Ahuja's book and NCERT books of Sociology for Class XI and XII.

Ethics: NCERT book on Psychology (for reference); Some Books of good authors, general reading habit would be of immense help. A brief Idea of Indian Philosophy including Vedanta, Jainism and Buddhism; Philosophy of Gandhi, Nehru, Tagore, Ambedkar and Vivekananda; lexicon Book, G. Subbarao's book on ethics. Reference material on Ethics, Integrity and Aptitude.

Essay: General books, published by National book Trust and Publications Division, etc.

Current Affairs

Newspapers: 'The Hindu','Indian Express, 'Business Standard'.

Magazines: 'Yojana', 'Kurukshetra', 'Chronicle' 'Frontline', Economic Political Weekly (EPW) 'India Year book', published by the Government of India. Latest economic and Social Welfare schemes of Government of India.

Websites

www.india.gov.in, www.newsonair.com, www.pib.nic.in, www.mrunal.org, www.insightsonindia.com, www.unacademy.in, www.mygov.in, www.PRSindia.org, wikipedia, Websites of various ministries of Government of India.

Radio and T.V.

All India Radio; D.D News; Rajya Sabha T.V., Lok Sabha T.V.

T.V serials: 'Satyamev Jayte', 'Yes Minister', 'Pradhanmantri', 'Samvidhan' and 'Bharat: Ek Khoj' (in leisurely time).

In addition to the above mentioned books, study in your leisurely time some good and authentic books on the subjects: Indian and International Politics, Administration, Society, Economics, Polity and Contemporary History for developing a good understanding and perspective. Amartya Sen, Ramchandra Guha, Gurcharan Das, Jean Dreze, Rajni Kothari, Shyamcharan Dubey, Kaushik Basu, Jagdish Bhagvati, Sunil Khilnani, Pratap Bhanu Mehta, Nandan Neilkeni, Shashi Tharoor, and P.Sainath are some notable authors, who have written on these subjects. Keep in mind, it is not compulsory to read all the above authors, read two or three books according to your interest. You will love to read it.

It is believed that during the preparations of the Civil Services examination, it is not necessary to know 'what to study',but it is obligatory to know 'what not to study'. In this context, my suggestion is that you should avoid reading the unauthentic and second grade study materials. Utilize the books of authentic authors and publishers, magazines, radio, T.V and websites of the Government of India to the best.

Besides this, never limit yourself to these books or magazines only. In this age of information, maximize the worthy use of internet by visiting the resourceful websites. At the same time, follow the All India Radio, BBC, D.D. News, Rajya Sabha T.V. etc., as they are the best available options. By watching the episodes of some of the famous serials: 'Yes Minister' 'Pradhanmantri', 'Samvidhan' and 'Satyamev Jayte' on TV, you can learn many good things.

In the end, while discussing the strategy of 'how to study', I would reiterate that there is no single way of doing the preparations. The ways and preparation strategies adopted by each aspirant can be different. However, you may adopt the following strategies while preparing for the Civil services examination:

1. Read a single subject or topic from one study material. Try to minimize the study materials, instead of maximizing it. Any failure in doing so would make the revision difficult and time consuming.
2. A timely revision of the syllabus is quite important in the preparations of Civil Services examination. Therefore, decide the topics which you would like to revise just before the exam. A weekly revision is important for retaining the things you have learnt.
3. Pen down the sources of the covered topics in a notebook or diary. This will be extremely helpful in the regular revisions and pre-exam revision.
4. Form the habit of making brief notes. If it is not possible, then underline or highlight the main points in the study materials itself.

5. Keeping the clippings of the important articles of the newspapers/magazines in a file is a good option, because it is not possible to re-read the newspapers and magazines.
6. If you get the conceptual clarity of some of the topics in one reading, it is not necessary to revise them.
7. You can comprehend the important study materials in two or three phases. The First phase can be a cursory and interesting reading of the study materials; the second can be a detailed study of those materials by highlighting the important points; and the third phase can be an analysis of the topic-related questions, in which you have to search their dimensions and interrelation with the rest of the syllabus. You must do the Group Discussions regularly to consolidate your learning.
8. The benefit of 'Group Discussion' is that while discussing it, we memorize the topic to an extent. Try to have the discussion in a small group. Don't be a passive participant in the discussions, explain the topic to the other members of the group. This practice can make you an expert of the topic.
9. Keep writing regularly along with the reading. Whatever you are writing, try to get inputs on it from some seniors or teachers, so that your writing gets improved regularly. You can participate in the 'Test Series' also to get a conceptual insight.
10. You need to study less, but your study should be well. Ample study materials are available in the market, but there is no need to get influenced and confused by them. Select the right materials according to the requirements of each subject. Read and write the topics, till you get a conceptual clarity. In this manner, you can definitely achieve the desired success in the Civil Services examination.

❑❑

5 Preliminary Examination: The First Step towards Success

As we know, preliminary examination is the first step towards achieving the success in the Civil Services Examination and the State Public Service Commission Examinations. You can appear in the Mains examination after clearing the Preliminary examination only. Therefore, clearing the prelims exam is the basic condition to progress ahead in this prestigious examination.

As per my experience, this phase of the examination is the most unpredictable and difficult phase. It is extremely difficult to predict the pattern of examination in this phase, i.e., you cannot guess the number of questions from a particular section or topic of General Studies. You cannot guess the safe cut-off score. You cannot even assess, whether you will come around that cut-off or not. It is difficult, not because you cannot prepare, but because you have to face the maximum competition in this phase.

An interesting fact about the preliminary examination is that, though many toppers have cleared this stage by a minimum margin, i.e., secured just a few marks more than the cut-off,but in the final score, they secured good ranks. In this regard,you need to keep one thing in mind that, though your fate will play a considerable role in this examination as well as in all the examinations of your life, but taking this phase lightly can be detrimental to your prospects in it.

Do not take Risk in this Phase

In this phase, about eight to nine lakhs aspirants apply per year; about four to five lakhs aspirants appear in the examination; while only a few thousands aspirants (generally 12-13 times against the total vacancy) get selected for appearing in the Mains exam. Therefore, carelessness in this stage can prove to be harmful for you. Hence, the better and the safer option is that, you should make such a strategy for the preparations of the Prelims examination, so that you may clear this phase with a comfortable margin.

Preliminary Examination : Scheme and Syllabus

We know that the Preliminary examination is an objective type exam. It is conducted in two shifts on a single day. These is a provision of 1/3 negative marking in this phase.

The General Studies consisting of 100 questions of 200 marks, is the first question paper; and the C-SAT, consisting of 80 questions of 200 marks is the second paper. After the year 2015, the marks obtained in the second paper, are not included for the merit of the prelims exam. Second paper is a qualifying paper. The syllabus of the prelims exam is as follows:

General Studies: Paper-I

1. Current events of national and international importance.
2. History of India and Indian National movement.
3. Indian and World Geography: the physical/social and economic geography of India and the world.
4. Indian polity and governance, constitution, political system, Panchayati Raj, public policy, Right issues etc.
5. Economic and social development, Sustainable development, poverty, inclusion, demographics and social sector initiatives etc.
6. General issues on environmental ecology, bio-diversity and climate change(that do not require subject specialization).
7. General science.

General Studies: Paper-II (C-SAT)

1. Comprehension.
2. Inter-personal skills, including communication skills.
3. Logical Reasoning and Analytical ability.
4. Decision making and problem solving.
5. General mental ability.
6. Basic numeracy (numbers and its relation, order of magnitude etc.-class 10th level), Data interpretation (charts, graphs, tables, data sufficiency etc.-class 10th level).

Dimensions of the Overall Preparations for Preliminary Examination

- Try to comprehend and remember the things studied by you. Mere memorizing it will not help. Still, there are certain things, which you have to memorize, i.e., the Fundamental Rights from Section 14 to 32 of Indian Constitution.
- The tendency of being a good learner always helps you in your life. Further, it is important especially for the prelims exam. Try to learn from every person or every source,e.g.,the advertisements of various government schemes, displayed in the Metro train or aired on F.M. Radio. Sometimes, information on such government schemes are asked in the multiple choice questions. Similarly, be aware of the news presented in the India Year Book, Yojana, P.I.B. and A.I.R. etc. In short, keep your eyes and ears open, as the preparations for one section of the General Studies can be useful in some other sections too. Such a diverse study and awareness helps a lot in this phase of examination.
- Focus on the sections of Current Affairs, History and Indian Freedom Movement, Geography of India and the World, Indian polity and

Constitution, Economic Development and Environment etc., as it will help you not only in the Mains exam, but also in the Interview of the Civil Services Examination.

- Give a special attention to the current and contemporary events, related to all the sections of General studies, e.g., the contemporary achievements and technological developments; the recent bills and amendments in the Constitution; ordinances; monetary policy; banking reforms; the impact of conferences on the climate change and endangered species and the conferences of the International organizations; and the news about any new geographical or cultural excavations.
- It is better to prepare well each and every section of General Studies. It is quite difficult to predict which segment of the General Studies, the maximum questions will be asked from. Sometimes, the maximum questions are asked from the Freedom Movement and Public Governance, and sometimes, most of the questions come from Geography and Environment. No one could have even thought that in the prelims exam of the year 2016, so many questions would be asked from the Current Affairs.
- Nevertheless, the preparations for the prelims exam cannot be limited to the current affairs only. There was a trend in the previous prelims exam that in the Paper-I, the basic questions of various sections of G.S were asked. In order to prepare thoroughly, you should study from the social sciences books of NCERT, meant for Class 9 to 12. (A detailed list of the books and sources is given in the chapter 'What to Study and What Not).
- Whatever you study in the current affairs, try to have a basic knowledge of the same,because very often in the prelims exam, the questions from the

current affairs are not straightforward,instead, they are linked with the traditional knowledge of the General Studies. Therefore, you should correlate the basic traditional knowledge with the contemporary events, while preparing for the prelims.

How to Prepare for General Studies - Paper-II (C-SAT)

The General Studies Paper-II is popularly known as C-SAT (Civil Services Aptitude Test). Though, it has become just a qualifying paper, but you can clear the prelims exam only after scoring the passing marks in this paper.

In fact, this paper is a test of the aptitude of an aspirant,in which the various skills and qualities of an aspirant are tested. It also tests the applicant's comprehension ability, communication skill, logical ability, analytical ability, mental ability and statistical aptitude etc. In order to clear this test, you need to have a fundamental clarity in the mathematics, statistics, reasoning and comprehension.

In the examination, many questions are asked from the comprehension. In order to solve these questions correctly, you must have the ability to read and comprehend quickly and give the apt answers. Hence at the preparation level, you should do the maximum reading, and improve the speed of your reading and comprehending. Besides, you need not be afraid of the Mathematics and the Reasoning sections, because only the basic level questions are asked in the examination.

For the preparations of the General Studies Paper-II, you should devote the major portion of your preparation in practice. Do not take this paper lightly. Rather, you should increase your capability level, so that you can score the cut-off marks with a fair margin.

Practice will Make Your Path Easier

You should give the utmost importance to the practice to improve the reading speed in both the papers of General

Studies, as it increases not only your reading and writing speed but alsoyour alertness. It also helps in minimizing the negative marking. Therefore, do practice, after doing your basic preparations.

While doing this, practise the papers of previous years (especially the papers of last five years). These papers can be quite helpful to you, as going through these papers, you can get an idea of the examination trend, and thus, can boost up your confidence.

Besides this, you can participate in a test series, or practise it at home with the help of the objective - type paper, available online or in the market. There is no other substitute for the practice; therefore, keep practising. After solving a paper, find their correct answers; and include these answers in your preparation materials, so that you can revise these answers, while studying the materials. In this way, you can cover important aspects of the exam.

How to Tackle the Negative Marking?

It is important to handle the negative marking in the prelims exam; and it can be done only through the practice. You should never think that you have to solve all the questions being asked in the paper, as it is practically not possible to know the correct answers of all the questions in the paper.

I advise you that, in the first round, try to solve those questions, which you are confident about. You should keep in mind that there may be many questions in the paper which you will not feel confident about; or in some questions, there will be a situation of 50-50. The most effective way of solving such questions is the 'Elimination Method', i.e., cross the options which are definitely incorrect. If after doing so two options are still remaining, then you can take the risk of ticking one option as correct.

Some aspirants are so scared of the negative marking, that they attempt very less questions. This is not a wise choice. Therefore, try to attempt reasonably good number of questions.

There is no thumb rule for the number of questions to be attempted in the prelims exam. It depends upon the level of that question paper and your preparation and knowledge. In short, handling of the negative marking in the examination is an art, which can be perfected through a continuous practice of solving the test papers.

Just before the Preliminary Examination

We have already discussed the importance of qualifying the preliminary examination. Let us discuss the ways to handle the tough time just before the examination and to succeed in it:

- First of all, stop thinking that you tend to forget the things you have studied earlier. Remain calm, and you will be able to remember and recollect them. The things which you have studied throughout the year, get saved in your memory; and when the need arises, you will be able to recall them definitely.
- Be confident that your preparation is up to the mark. If you remain confident, the chance of your success increases. Remember,out of lakhs of aspirants appearing in Civil Services examination, only few aspirants are able to maintain their level of confidence.
- The principle of 'Nishkaam Karmayoga' (disinterested action) will help you a lot during the prelims exam. Write the examination without taking stress of its outcome. Most of the aspirants, who have failed to clear the prelims exam, have accepted that, despite of knowing the right answers, they have selected the wrong options and have filled the wrong circles due to the tension, stress or the haste.
- Do revise. It is not the proper time to study the new things. If possible, do one more revision of sections of polity, geography, economy, environment and current affairs.

- For handling the negative marking,a continuous practice is essential. Therefore, solve the test papers;have an understanding of the calculation in the negative marking; and form an effective strategy for it.
- Do practice both the papers, i.e., Paper-I and Paper-II.
- The examination is conducted in the morning session, therefore prior to the examination, try to form the habit of sleeping on time and waking up early, so that on the day of the examination you can wake up with a fresh mind.
- Never neglect your sleep hours by imitating someone, and sleep at least for seven hours.
- Eat light and digestive food, like fruits, vegetables and salad.
- Walk for about half an hour in a park in the morning or evening.
- Have faith in God as well as in yourself.
- Avoid unnecessary things and negativity.

In the Examination Hall

- One mistake, which we all commit during the prelims exam, is that we do not read the questions carefully or attentively. Sometimes, in a multiple choice question, Due to being careless or in a hurry, we do not pay attention to the actual meaning of the question; and, instead of marking the incorrect answer, we mark the correct answer and lose the marks. Therefore, read every question and its each word carefully.
- The prelims paper is set both in the Hindi as well as in the English language. If you are unable to comprehend any word or sentence in one language, do see its translation in the other language, if possible. By doing so, you may get some important 'clues', which can help you in

comprehending that word or sentence and writing the correct answer.

- Do read the instructions given on the first page of the question paper. You are asked to fill the circle with black ballpoint pen only. Fill the circles as per the instructions.
- After having an overall view of the paper, you are able to guess the level of the questions in the paper. Some aspirants start panicking after finding thequestions tough. I would like to remind such aspirants that the level (whether easy or tough) is same for all the aspirants. Therefore, do not panic, and give your best performance with your full capability.
- Some aspirants are so anxious, that they start looking for the correct answers of the first paper, even before the second paper begins. It is completely unadvisable. Forget about the first paper till the second paper ends. Try to relax, and appear in the second paper with a fresh mind.
- Do not start looking for the answer key just after finishing the papers. If you really want to know the correct answers, match your answers with a good answer key after some days. You must also keep this fact in your mind, that none of the answer key is completely correct, so without bothering about the cut-off of the prelims exam, start preparing for the mains exam with full dedication.

❑❑

6

How to Perform Well in the 'Mains Exam'?

It would not be an exaggeration, if it is said that the second phase of the Mains Examination is the path, which can lead an aspirant to become a topper in the Civil Services examination. In fact, this examination plays a pivotal role in the making of your final merit. It plays a decisive role, and decides whether you will be selected or not; and if you get selected, then what would be your rank. Therefore, start the preparations for the Mains exam along with the preparations of the Prelims exam.This examination should not be neglected at any cost in the whole process of your preparations for the Civil Services Examination.

Scheme and Syllabus of the Mains Examination

The final merit list of Civil Services Examinations is prepared out of 2025 marks, in which the mains exam carries 1750 marks. It means the Mains exam has a weightage of about 86% of the total merit.

The Mains exam generally continues for about a week, and it comprises nine papers. Out of the nine papers, the marks of only the seven papers are included in the final merit, and the remaining two papers (compulsary languages) are qualifying in nature.

Out of the two papers of Compulsory Languages, the first paper is of English, and the second paper is of any one language out of 22 Indian languages mentioned in the Eighth Schedule of the Constitution of India. Both these papers are of 300 marks and the marks obtained in these two papers are not added in the final merit.

Papers to be counted for merit

Paper-I
Essay **250 Marks**
Paper-II
General Studies I **250 Marks**
(Indian Heritage and Culture, History and Geography of the World and Society)
Paper-III
General Studies II **250 Marks**
(Governance, Constitution, Polity, Social Justice and International relations)
Paper-IV
General Studies III **250 Marks**
(Technology, Economic Development, Bio-diversity, Environment, Security and Disaster Management)
Paper-V
General Studies IV **250 Marks**
(Ethics, Integrity and Aptitude)
Paper-VI
Optional Subject-Paper 1 **250 Marks**
Paper-VII
Optional Subject-Paper 2 **250 Marks**
Sub Total (Written test) 1750 Marks
Personality Test 275 Marks
Grand Total 2025 Marks

Main Examination

The Main Examination is intended to assess the overall intellectual traits and depth of understanding of candidates rather than merely the range of their information and memory.

The nature and standard of questions in the General Studies papers (Paper II to Paper V) will be such that a well-educated person will be able to answer them without any specialized study. The questions will be such as to test a candidate's general awareness of a variety of subjects, which will have relevance for a career in Civil Services. The questions are likely to test the candidate's basic understanding of all relevant issues and ability to analyze and take a view on conflicting socio-economic goals, objectives and demands. The candidates must give relevant, meaningful and succinct answers.

The scope of the syllabus for optional subject papers (Paper VI and Paper VII) for the examination is broadly of the honours degree level i.e. a level higher than the bachelors' degree and lower than the masters' degree. In the case of Engineering, Medical Science and law, the level corresponds to the bachelors' degree.

Syllabi of the papers included in the scheme of Civil Services (Main) Examination are given as follows:-

QUALIFYING PAPERS ON INDIAN LANGUAGES AND ENGLISH

The aim of the paper is to test the candidates ability to read and understand serious discursive prose, and express his ideas clearly and correctly, in English and Indian Language concerned.

The pattern of questions would be broadly as follows:

(i) Comprehension of given passages
(ii) Precis Writing
(iii) Usage and Vocabulary
(iv) Short Essays

Indian Languages:

(i) Comprehension of given passages
(ii) Precis Writing
(iii) Usage and Vocabulary
(iv) Short Essays
(v) Translation from English to the Indian language and vice-versa.

Note 1: The Papers on Indian Languages and English will be of Matriculation or equivalent standard and will be of qualifying nature only. The marks obtained in these papers will not be counted for ranking.

Note 2: The candidates will have to answer the English and Indian Languages papers in English and the respective Indian language (except where translation is involved).

PAPER-I

Essay: Candidates may be required to write essays on multiple topics. They will be expected to keep closely to the subject of the essay to arrange their ideas in orderly fashion and to write concisely. Credit will be given for effective and exact expression.

PAPER-II

General Studies- I: Indian Heritage and Culture, History and Geography of the World and Society.

- Indian culture will cover the salient aspects of Art Forms, Literature and Architecture from ancient to modern times.
- Modern Indian history from about the middle of the eighteenth century until the present- significant events, personalities, issues
- The Freedom Struggle-its various stages and important contributors/contributions from different parts of the country.
- Post-independence consolidation and reorganization within the country.
- History of the world will include events from 18th century such as industrial revolution, world wars, redrawal of national boundaries, colonization, decolonization, political philosophies like communism, capitalism, socialism etc.-their forms and effect on the society.
- Salient features of Indian Society, Diversity of India.
- Role of women and women's organization, population and associated issues, poverty

and developmental issues, urbanization, their problems and their remedies.

- Effects of globalization on Indian society
- Social empowerment, communalism, regionalism & secularism.
- Salient features of world's physical geography.
- Distribution of key natural resources across the world (including South Asia and the Indian sub-continent); factors responsible for the location of primary, secondary, and tertiary sector industries in various parts of the world (including India)
- Important Geophysical phenomena such as earthquakes, Tsunami, Volcanic activity, cyclone etc., geographical features and their location-changes in critical geographical features (including water-bodies and ice-caps) and in flora and fauna and the effects of such changes.

PAPER-III

General Studies- II: Governance, Constitution, Polity, Social Justice and International relations.

- Indian Constitution- historical underpinnings, evolution, features, amendments, significant provisions and basic structure.
- Functions and responsibilities of the Union and the States, issues and challenges pertaining to the federal structure, devolution of powers and finances up to local levels and challenges therein.
- Separation of powers between various organs dispute redressal mechanisms and institutions.
- Comparison of the Indian constitutional scheme with that of other countries
- Parliament and State Legislatures-structure, functioning, conduct of business, powers & privileges and issues arising out of these.
- Structure, organization and functioning of the Executive and the Judiciary; Ministries and

Departments of the Government; pressure groups and formal/informal associations and their role in the Polity.

- Salient features of the Representation of People's Act.
- Appointment to various Constitutional posts, powers, functions and responsibilities of various Constitutional Bodies.
- Statutory, regulatory and various quasi-judicial bodies
- Government policies and interventions for development in various sectors and issues arising out of their design and implementation.
- Development processes and the development industry- the role of NGOs, SHGs, various groups and associations, donors, charities, institutional and other stakeholders
- Welfare schemes for vulnerable sections of the population by the Centre and States and the performance of these schemes; mechanisms, laws, institutions and Bodies constituted for the protection and betterment of these vulnerable sections.
- Issues relating to development and management of Social Sector/Services relating to Health, Education, Human Resources.
- Issues relating to poverty and hunger.
- Important aspects of governance, transparency and accountability, e-governance- applications, models, successes, limitations, and potential; citizens charters, transparency & accountability and institutional and other measures.
- Role of civil services in a democracy.
- India and its neighborhood- relations.
- Bilateral, regional and global groupings and agreements involving India and/or affecting India's interests

- Effect of policies and politics of developed and developing countries on India's interests, Indian diaspora.
- Important International institutions, agencies and fora- their structure, mandate.

PAPER-IV

General Studies-III: Technology, Economic Development, Biodiversity, Environment, Security and Disaster Management.

- Indian Economy and issues relating to planning, mobilization of resources, growth, development and employment.
- Inclusive growth and issues arising from it.
- Government Budgeting.
- Major crops cropping patterns in various parts of the country, different types of irrigation and irrigation systems storage, transport and marketing of agricultural produce and issues and related constraints; e-technology in the aid of farmers
- Issues related to direct and indirect farm subsidies and minimum support prices; Public Distribution System- objectives, functioning, limitations, revamping; issues of buffer stocks and food security; Technology missions; economics of animal-rearing.
- Food processing and related industries in India- scope and significance, location, upstream and downstream requirements, supply chain management.
- Land reforms in India.
- Effects of liberalization on the economy, changes in industrial policy and their effects on industrial growth.
- Infrastructure: Energy, Ports, Roads, Airports, Railways etc.

- Investment models.
- Science and Technology-developments and their applications and effects in everyday life
- Achievements of Indians in science & technology; indigenization of technology and developing new technology.
- Awareness in the fields of IT, Space, Computers, robotics, nano-technology, bio-technology and issues relating to intellectual property rights.
- Conservation, environmental pollution and degradation, environmental impact assessment
- Disaster and disaster management.
- Linkages between development and spread of extremism.
- Role of external state and nonstate actors in creating challenges to internal security.
- Challenges to internal security through communication networks, role of media and social networking sites in internal security challenges, basics of cyber security; money-laundering and its prevention
- Security challenges and their management in border areas; linkages of organized crime with terrorism
- Various Security forces and agencies and their mandate

PAPER-V

General Studies- IV: Ethics, Integrity and Aptitude

This paper will include questions to test the candidates' attitude and approach to issues relating to integrity, probity in public life and his problem solving approach to various issues and conflicts faced by him in dealing with society. Questions may utilise the case study approach to determine these aspects. The following broad areas will be covered.

- **Ethics and Human Interface:** Essence, determinants and consequences of Ethics in human actions; dimensions of ethics; ethics in private and public relationships. Human Values - lessons from the lives and teachings of great leaders, reformers and administrators; role of family, society and educational institutions in inculcating values.

- Attitude: content, structure, function; its influence and relation with thought and behaviour; moral and political attitudes; social influence and persuasion.
- Aptitude and foundational values for Civil Services; integrity, impartiality and non-partisanship, objectivity, dedication to public service, empathy, tolerance and compassion towards the weaker-sections.
- Emotional intelligence-concepts and their utilities and application in administration and governance.
- Contributions of moral thinkers and philosophers from India and world.
- Public/Civil service values and Ethics in Public administration: Status and problems; ethical concerns and dilemmas in government and private institutions; laws, rules, regulations and conscience as sources of ethical guidance; accountability and ethical governance; strengthening of ethical and moral values in governance; ethical issues in international relations and funding; corporate governance.
- Probity in Governance: Concept of public service; Philosophical basis of governance and probity; Information sharing and transparency in government, Right to Information, Codes of Ethics, Codes of Conduct, Citizen's Charters, Work culture, Quality of service delivery, Utilization of public funds, challenges of corruption.
- Case Studies on above issues.

PAPER-VI & PAPER VII

Optional Subject Papers I & II

Candidates may choose any optional subject from amongst the list of Optional Subjects.

Understanding Topper's Marks Obtained in Mains Exam

Undoubtedly, the mains exam plays a crucial role for an aspirant to become a topper in the civil services examination. Before learning how to prepare for the Mains exam, it would be better to understand the arithmetic of the marks obtained by the various toppers in its different papers, so that you can prepare a strategy according to your needs. For this, we will do a brief analysis by comparing the marks scored by some of the aspirants, who have become the toppers in the new pattern of the civil services examination, and will try reach to a conclusion.

For example, Gaurav Agrawal, the first rank holder in the Civil Services Examination, 2013, obtained 135 marks in Essay, 338 marks in General Studies, and 296 marks in the Optional Subject. Overall, he got 769 marks out of 1750 marks of the mains exam, which is about 44 percent score.

Ira Singhal, the first rank holder in the Civil Services Examination, 2014, obtained 160 marks in Essay, 455 marks in General Studies, and 305 marks in the Optional Subject. Overall, she obtained 920 marks (about 52 percent) in the mains exam.

I, Nishant Jain, secured the thirteenth Rank, and obtained 160 marks in Essay, 378 marks in General Studies (124 marks in Ethics) and 313 marks in the Optional Subject. In this way, the score of my Mains exam was 851 marks, i.e., about 49 percent.

Tina Dabi, the Civil Services Topper, 2015, obtained 145 marks in Essay, 424 marks in General Studies, 299 marks in the Optional Subject. Her total score in the mains exam was 868 marks (about 50 percent).

Nandini KR, topper of 2016 exam obtained 142 marks in essay, 454 marks in General Studies and 331 marks in optional subject. Her total score in the mains exam was 927 marks (about 53%).

From the above data, we have an overall idea of the marks obtained by the five toppers in the previous four civil services examination; and we come to know many important points, i.e.,firstly, the toppers' score in the mains exam is around 50 percent; secondly, during the last four years, the papers of Essay, Ethics (G.S. Paper-IV) and the Optional Subject have emerged as the important pillars of success.

Hence, more focus should be given to the papers, like Optional Subject, Essay, Ethics, and the General Studies. Instead of depending on the marks in the interview, try to obtain good marks in the Mains exam itself. There are many aspirants, who topped the civil services examination by scoring excellent marks in the Mains exam, despite of obtaining less mark in the interview.

For a ready reference, I am sharing my marksheet of the Civil Services examination, 2014, as given below:

UPSC CSE Main Exam, 2014

Essay: 160 marks/250
General Studies Paper-I: 89 marks /250
General Studies Paper-II: 88 marks/250
General Studies Paper-III: 77 marks/250
General Studies Paper-IV: 124 marks/250
Optional Subject- Hindi Literature Paper-I: 166 marks/250
Optional Subject-Hindi Literature Paper-II: 147 marks/250
Total marks: 851 marks/1750

UP PCS Mains Exam, 2014

General Hindi:94 marks/150
Essay:110 marks/ 150

General Studies Paper-I: 121 marks/200
General Studies Paper-II: 145 marks/200
Optional Subject- Hindi Literature Paper-I: 157.64 marks/200
Optional Subject- Hindi Literature Paper-II: 140.93 marks/200
Optional Subject- Social Work Paper-I: 138.83 marks/200
Optional Subject- Social WorkPaper-II: 145.74 marks/200
Total marks: 1053.14 marks/1500

Just after the Preliminary Examination

After appearing in the prelims exam, some aspirants start preparing for the mains exam, while some remain in the dilemma, whether they will be able to clear the prelims exam or not. I would like to tell you a practical solution for getting over this dilemma. If you are confident that you will clear the prelims exam,then start preparing for the mains exam without any delay; and if unfortunately, you feel that you will not be able to clear the prelim exam this time, then also start preparing for the mains exam for the next year. I mean to say that, whether you qualify in the prelims exam or not, you have to continue the preparations for the mains exam. Some important points are discussed below:

- Do not bother about the various answer keys available in the market, just relax for some time, and start preparing for the mains exam directly.
- In order to fetch a good score, one must do two things. Firstly, develop a good writing skill and secondly, revise. It hardly matters whether you write for an hour or half an hour, the important thing is to keep writing. The preparations of the Essay paper does not demand much time, and it helps you in getting good marks. Therefore, my suggestion is that try to write at least one or two essays per week in the designated time-frame.
- The same thing can be done while doing the case studies of the Ethics paper. Practice at least 2-3 model case studies per week.

- It is very important for the Mains exam to have a deep understanding of the current affairs. In the prelims exam of 2016, many questions were asked from the Current Affairs. Therefore, keep yourself updated by reading the newspapers, good monthly magazines, radio and websites of Government of India.
- Whenever you are free or feeling bored, you may watch the episodes of the serials, like 'Pradhanmantri', 'Samvidhan' and 'Satyamev Jayte'.
- Do the revision of the Social Sciences book from Class IX to XII published by NCERT. The various important books, like Spectrum's book on 'Modern India', M. Laxmikanth's book on 'Indian Polity' and 'Indian Governance', 'Post-Independent India' for contemporary history, economic survey, geography, and NCERT's book on Environment also must be revised.
- Be in continuous touch with the websites, like mrunal.org, insightsonindia.com, newsonair.com and pib.nic.in etc.
- You should try to test your learning level from time to time; and for this, writing the test series is a good method. Give tests of the subjects, like General Studies and Optional Subject. Do go through the model answers of the test series, and prepare them. Do not join multiple test series at one time.
- Keep your full focus on the Mains exam,instead of focusing on the interview or on the next prelims exam. You will get a sufficient time for their preparations afterwards.
- Increase your writing speed (while maintaining the legibility), so that you can attempt all the questions in the paper of the Mains exam. Never try to cross the prescribed word limit.

- Make a diary and start writing the topics, which you have studied on that day; and also write down the sources from where you have studied it. It will be helpful during your exam days.
- Performing well in the Optional Subject makes the path of your success much easier. Therefore, try to give the maximum time to your Optional Subject, after the prelims exam and till the beginning of the mains exam. Keep revising it.
- Every aspirant has his/her own way of studying or preparing the examination strategy. Therefore, neither take the stress, nor get extremely influenced by the other aspirants.
- Those aspirants, who had already appeared in the mains exam in the previous year but had not been able to qualify it, should not think that they would not be able to clear the exam this time also. Give the exam with full enthusiasm; stay stress free; and learn from the mistakes committed earlier.

Filling up the form for Mains Examination: Things to be kept in Mind

After qualifying the prelims exam,you are required to fill a Detailed Application Form (DAF) for appearing in the Mains examination. It is a very important document, as it will be used by the Interview Board to gather the basic information about you. In this form, you need to fill the information, like your name, home district, home state, mother tongue, community, category, educational and professional qualifications, interests, experience, optional subject, achievements and preferences of service and cadre.

In my opinion, this form must be filled calmly and diligently, because you cannot change any information given in it, after getting the interview call. Further, your service and cadre will be allotted on the basis of this form.

While filling up such an important form, you should take the following precautions:

- Firstly, never fill up this form in a hurry. Do not make mistakes while writing the numbers or spelling the words.
- Never give a false or misleading information.
- You can choose the centre of the Mains exam, hence select the centre of your choice from the given centre list.
- The medium of the Mains exam, and the medium of the interview, can be different,e.g., if you have written the Mains exam in the English medium, you can give the interview in the Hindi medium, if you opt for it. Any one of the 22 Indian languages, mentioned in the Constitution of India and English, can be your language medium. Therefore, select the language medium for the Mains exam and Interview according to your convenience.
- Give a detailed description of your educational qualifications (secondary and higher education) and experience, e.g., in the subject column, do write all the subjects studied by you at the 10th and 12th class. You have to give the details of your jobs too, if you have done any in the government/ private sector previously, or if you are doing it at present also.
- In the Question No. 18 of the DAF, you have to give the complete details of the awards, medals, scholarships, if you have won any. Apart from this, you have to give the details of sports or N.C.C. training, if you have done any. You must give the details of your achievements and positions, held by you in your school and college. You must write in the form about the co-curricular activities and interests you have, as many questions from this portion may be asked in the Interview. The 18(d) column in the form is the most important one,

because it asks about your 'other co-curricular activities and subjects of interest' (hobbies). So write in this column, not only about your hobbies, but also about your co-curricular activities and interests.

- I find that most of the aspirants are confused in filling this column. You should give the name of only that hobby,which you have been really associated with, because the Interview Board can easily find out the fact, whether you are really interested in this field or not. For example, you may write your areas of interest, like reading stories/novels, watching movies, debates/theatre or playing cricket, cooking etc., Besides, do not write any fictitious or impractical hobby.
- Regarding filling up your preferences for the service and cadre, I would suggest you to fill up this column very carefully, since your service and cadre becomes very important, after qualifying the Civil Services examination. While filling up your preferences, try to know the profile of each and every service. For this, you can visit the web site of DOPT, or take the help of your seniors. It is important that you decide your priorities on the basis of your interest, ability and profile of the preferred service. For the I.A.S and I.P.S services, you are required to fill up the cadre preferences too. Generally, the aspirants decide the cadre on the basis of the geographical and cultural proximity. My suggestion is that, while deciding the cadre, gather a brief information about the administrative culture of that state cadre and then decide.

Overall Preparations for the Mains Examination: Some Important Tips

- A new pattern has been included in the mains exam from the year-2013. Therefore, you should go carefully through the question papers of Mains exam from 2013 onwards. Comprehend the papers; and keep referring them, whenever and wherever needed. After studying and analyzing the previous papers, you will gradually understand the trend of questions being asked in the Mains exam.

- It is not possible to score good marks without improving the writing skill. Therefore, for improving your writing skill, you must devote sufficient time on the writing practice. Write at least one essay and two case studies of Ethics every week. Realizing its importance, I have devoted a separate chapter for it, 'Writing Skill: The Basis of Success'.
- I have noticed, that there are a few important qualities in an aspirant, which make him/her a topper and different from the other aspirants. Out of these qualities, the level of competence on the language medium is the most important quality. It hardly matters whether you select the English/ Hindi or any other Indian language from the 22 languages offered in the syllabus as the medium of the examination, what matters is the level of your competence in the opted language; as it helps you in expressing yourself clearly. You must keep in mind that, when we talk about the competence in a language, it does not mean that you should use a literary, poetic or decorative language in the exam. It means that you should use a simple and natural language in the examination, which is comprehensible to the examiner. A detailed discussion on this topic has been done in the chapter, 'Significance of having command over your language'.
- I have already discussed that, for excellent performance in the mains exam, our approach

should be integrated and broad. Besides, you must possess the ability to view things and events in relation to each other,especially the understanding of the traditional knowledge in the General Studies, with relation to the contemporary developments, can improve your answers to a great extent. Therefore, during the preparations for the Mains exam, keep updating your traditional knowledge with relation to the current affairs,e.g., judicial reforms or the administrative and police reforms and their respective status in the present times.

- During the preparations of the Mains examination, you must always keep in mind that, you should give due importance to all the papers, and should not make any paper your weak point. It is practically not possible that all the papers, attempted by you, go perfect. So, even if you do not score the best, try to score better, at least in all the papers.
- Give your special focus on the papers of the previous years of the Mains examination,i.e., from the year 2013 to the current year. The practice of going through the papers again and again will let you understand the nature and trend of the papers of General Studies, Essay and Optional Subject.
- It is a good option, if you join any good test series for doing the practice of writing the relevant answers in the Mains exam in the prescribed time limit. While doing this, you should go through the answers of the questions asked in the test series after writing the test,as it helps in your preparations. Pay attention to the important suggestions for writing a better answer, and keep improving yourself by doing the test series. However, the opinion of the examiner of the test series may differ from the opinion of the examiner

of the Civil Services Exam. There are some aspirants, who used to get the average marks in the test series,but they performed very well in the Mains exam.Therefore, always remain positive and confident.

- Now-a-days in the Mains examination, you are supposed to write the answers of the questions of General Studies in 200 words only. Therefore, learn the art of expressing yourself in brief. It means that even if you know four-five points only about a question, try to write a good answer;if you know more, then try to refine your answer; but avoid writing the irrelevant things in the examination.

How to Prepare the Compulsory Languages Papers?

The compulsory language papers is of a qualifying nature, but sometimes, the aspirants fail to qualify it. As a result, the answer sheets of the rest of the papers are not evaluated. Although, you need not prepare very hard for the two compulsory language papers, but you need to pay some attention to these papers.

As far as the Hindi paper is concerned, the paper is comprised of a short essay of 600 words; the questions based on the portions of an unseen passage; summary of a passage; translation of a passage from English to Hindi and vice-versa; and some questions from the vocabulary, e.g., proverbs-idioms, homonyms, synonyms and correct form of the sentences etc.

Often, it is noticed that the aspirants, who have been out of touch with the reading and writing in Hindi for the past few years(due to study, job or some other reasons), face problems in Hindi while reading the newspapers with speed or writing without any grammatical errors., though the questions are of the level of 10th standard. I would suggest to such aspirants, especially those who are appearing in the exam with the English medium and have selected Hindi as their Compulsory Indian Language, to practice the reading and writing of Hindi along with the overall preparations. Be in constant touch with Hindi, so that you may not face any problem in the examination.

Try to judge the level of your competence in both the papers of the Compulsory Language; and accordingly analyze the efforts you need to put in for preparing these papers. A regular practice is required to prepare these papers.

How to Prepare the Papers of General Studies and Ethics: Useful Tips

The latest syllabus of the mains examination of the Civil Services is a little broad, but at the same time,it is immensely logical and dynamic. Several new sections have been added in it, like Internal Security, World History, World Geography, Contemporary History of the post-independent India, Indian Society and Ethics. The importance of General Studies increases due to the fact that its syllabus is inter-related and inter-connected. That is the reason it becomes interesting and meaningful.

Let us do a paper-wise discussion of the points, which must be kept in mind during the preparations; but before doing that, I would recommend to go through the paper of General Studies of the Mains exam from the year 2013 onwards. It will help you in understanding the nature, level and the new pattern of the exam.

The syllabus of all the four papers of General Studies is very broad and detailed. Keep reading the whole syllabus; and by covering its each and every section, make it the basis of your preparations for the mains examination. A list of the reference books and study materials has been given in the chapter 'Knowing What to Study and What Not'. Now, I would like to discuss the following points paper-wise, so that you can prepare for the examination thoroughly:

General Studies: Paper-I

Mainly, this paper includes the Indian and World History, Indian Culture and Heritage, World Geography and

Indian Society.Mostly, the traditional questions are asked in this paper. You must remember the following points for preparing this paper:

- Study Indian History in relation with the Indian Culture and Heritage.
- Prepare the section of 'Indian Freedom Struggle' very well.
- Do remember that in the revised syllabus, now you have to study the history of the post-independent India too.
- It is better to do some preparation of the section of 'Indian Society'.
- In Geography, do prepare the human geography well, along with the physical geography.
- Prepare the section of 'Natural Disasters' very well.

General Studies: Paper-II

Mainly, the questions from the Indian Governance and Indian Polity, Indian Constitution, Social Justice and International Relations are asked in this paper. Some important points for the Paper-II are given below:

- Read the two books, 'Indian Governance' and 'Indian Polity', written by M. Laxmikanth. You must read this book,'Indian Polity' again and again, but a quick reading of the book, 'Indian Governance' is sufficient. The section of 'Polity and Constitution' are very important for the Preliminary as well as for the Mains examination.
- The section of 'Social Justice' is very important. For preparing it, study the chapter,'Rights Related Issues', from M. Laxmikanth's book 'Indian Governance'.
- Prepare the section of 'Governance' very well. It will be helpful in Paper IV (Ethics) also.
- For preparing the International Relations, focus on the neighboring countries and the international organizations especially. The Current Affairs

is extremely important for preparing this section, because you can mention the relevant contemporary events in your answers.

General Studies: Paper-III

The questions, mainly related to the Economics and Economic Development, Technology, Environment and Bio-diversity, Security and Disaster Management are asked in this paper. The following are some important tips to prepare this paper:

- Current Affairs is very important for this paper. A glance at the question papers of previous years on the Economy and Economic Development reveals that the Civil Services Examination gives a special emphasis on the contemporary issues as well as on the traditional syllabus in this paper.
- One more trend, related to the questions on economy,is that the emphasis is being given on the economic as well as on the social aspects, e.g., the topics like Inclusive Development, Poverty, Employment, Hunger etc. are also there in the syllabus. In such a situation, it would be better to prepare in a holistic way.
- While answering the questions related to economy, do keep in mind the economic survey, the budget and the governmental policies. If required in your answers, give the facts of the 'Budget' and the governmental policies as the examples. It will give an edge to you over others. In some economic surveys at many places, the Indian Economy has been compared with the Economy of other countries. These comparative points can be incorporated in your answers.
- Issues related to the Agriculture and Land-reforms are also important.
- Some topics of Paper-II can be combined with the Paper-III.

- You need not worry much if you find yourself weak in the 'Science-Tech' section. You can have a quick reading of the book by Ashok Kumar and Vipul, published by Tata McGraw Hills. Environment and Disaster Management sections should also be prepared very well.

General Studies: Paper-IV

This paper, titled 'Ethics, Integrity and Aptitude', was introduced in the year 2013. Though this paper also carries 250 marks, as those of the other papers in the Mains examination, but still, it is considered to be very important. The main reason is its varied range of marks. You can score as high as 125 marks or more and as low as below 75 marks. In the mains examination, 2014, I scored 124 marks in the Ethics paper. I found that in this paper, aspirants can score very good marks which can improve their final score substantially.

The following are some tips to score well in this paper:

- This paper is divided into two sections. The first section comprises of the theoretical questions; and the second section comprises of the practical questions, in which you have to solve some case studies. Therefore, do keep in mind that during your preparations as well as in the examination hall, you have to devote an equal amount of time to both the sections, and give them equal importance.
- Try to read and comprehend well the technical terminology related to the Ethics, aptitude, emotional inlilligence etc., so that you can write the exact definition of these terms and make their correct use, whenever required. Some of the technical terms are: morality, good governance, transparency, honesty, accountability, attitude, aptitude, intelligence, integrity, sympathy, empathy, impartiality, tolerance, objectivity,

commitment, compassion, perseverance, emotional intelligence, reliability, conflict of interest and environmental ethics etc. For the terms related to Psychology, you can study the NCERT book.

- Generally, the questions related to the lives and teachings of the great leaders, reformers and administrators are also asked in this paper. Apart from this, the questions related to the contribution of moral thinkers and philosophers of India and the World are also asked.Since this section, to some extent, is related to Philosophy,I would suggest to prepare the practical teachings of Jain, Buddhist and the Gandhian Philosophy. In my opinion, you should pay a special attention to the thoughts of the Indian leaders/reformers, like Gandhiji, Nehru, Tagore, Dr. Ambedkar and Swami Vivekanada etc., and prepare well the topics on them.
- Give special attention to various systems of reforms in the public governance and laws. Try to have a good understanding of e-governance, citizen charter and Right to Information. Besides, understand the practical implications of these systems on the administration.
- There is no fixed formula for preparing this paper, as most of the questions in this paper are dynamic and practical. In order to answer them, a detailed study and personal experience is required. There are several questions which cannot be prepared from any book. You are required to answer such questions by using your personal instincts, and experience, e.g. the questions like, 'What is the definition of joy for you'?, and ' Which personality are you influenced with and why'?
- For preparing the Ethics paper, more importance should be given to the general 'reading habit' and

'observation'. Along with reading the textbooks, form a habit of reading the good books and magazines, like 'Reader's Digest' in your spare time.

- In this paper, a correct understanding and perception of the subject, along with studies and experience, develops the maturity level, and thus helps a lot. Your balanced, detailed and dynamic views and your inclusive and interdisciplinary approach will be reflected in your answers spontaneously.
- Practice is the key factor in solving the case studies. Try to solve two to four case studies weekly. Prepare the theoretical aspects of this paper too, since a case study is the applied form of a theory.
- Now the question is how to solve a case study. In this regard, I would suggest that, while studying the theoretical aspects (Section-I), develop some habits,i.e., looking the relevance of various decisions and facts from an ethical view, understanding the circumstances and pressures behind taking any unethical decision and applying and analyzing the theoretical aspects in life.
- Whenever you solve a case study, analyze the legal and ethical aspects of your suggestions. Generally, your answer must not be against the constitution and the law. There are certain issues in which an internal conflict arises between law and ethics. In my view, first preference should be given to the legal aspect and second preference to the ethical aspect.
- While solving the case study, do select the most suitable optionand its effect or other available ethical options and their expected outcome, but only after analyzing the circumstances prevailing during the event.

Improving Writing Skills

By learning the art of writing, you can improve your writing skills, and will be able to write the answers in the mains exam in an effective manner. The following are some important tips to improve your writing skills and succeed in the examination:

- Write an original answer in your own language and style. It means neither copy someone else's answers, nor write in a literary language or style. Here, the originality does not mean a creation of literature.
- Write your answer in totality, connecting different relevant aspects. Although you have to write your answer in 200 words only, but try to highlight the important aspects.
- You should be able to structure your answer. If you are supposed to write your answer in just 200 words, then in my opinion, structure your answer in the following manner:
  - Firstly, you should write two or three lines about the background of the topic;
  - Secondly, write two or three paragraphs as the main portion of the answer, as per the requirement;
  - Thirdly, highlight the various relevant aspects, while writing your answer;
  - At the end, write a conclusion to give a positive and futuristic solution to the issue asked in the question.
- Do not cross the word limit, otherwise you will not be able to complete the paper. In fact, there is nothing wrong in writing a short answer, even if it is short of the word limit by 20-25 words. If you have violated the word limit by a margin of 10-20 %, even then you need not worry.

- While writing the answers, especially in General Studies, write in the paragraph form, instead of using the point form. As far as writing the answers of General Studies is concerned, one cannot write the answers in flat 'yes' or 'no'. You should use the paragraphs if the question is analytical, and use the point form if the question is factual; but never write any answer with the help of the points only, use paragraphs too. In short, it is better to use paragraphs while writing an answer. If you feel the need of using some points, then you can obviously do it.
- Generally, the aspirants are advised to attempt all the questions. One general query is that how one should deal with the questions, whose answers are not known to them. There are several ways of dealing such a situation. For this, you must develop the 'writing skills'. You must start writing anyhow according to the demand of the question, and include your own points too from the topic's background. It has been discussed in detail in the chapter on 'Writing Skill: The basis of success'.
- Some aspirants want to know that what should be their approach while writing an answer. I personally believe that your every answer should be filled with suggestions and the hope of improvement, so that the examiner can form an idea of you as a bureaucrat, that you have the capability of bringing a positive change in the society. You can also discuss some scheme or programme in your answer, but you must have a prior knowledge of the pros and cons of that scheme or programme. Try to give a balanced view. Have the knowledge of both the negative and positive aspects of that issue, only then you will be able to present a balanced view.

- Always use your own common sense, no matter the others are giving much advice to you. By now, your rigorous studies, experience and preparations would have developed a better common sense in you; use it.
- Always keep in mind the demand and expectations of that particular question in the paper, while writing its answer. Deal the question separately, in accordance with its demand and expectations.
- Apart from this, your thought and thought process must be organized. Write your answer points in an organized manner. It will give an impression to the examiner that your thought process is well organized and systamatic.
- Write the theory portion in a nice manner. If something relevant is going on in the current situation, add it too in your answer. It makes your answer better, and it will fetch you good marks. In short, your answer should be relevant.

As far as the use of terminology is concerned, it should be simple, easy and comprehensible, but it should not appear like an informal talk. In fact, there is a natural difference between the written language and the spoken language. While talking informally, we do use an informal style and terminology, but while writing the same content, the language has to be a little refined and compact. However, there is no need to make your language and style literary or decorative.

What we should do some days before the Mains Examination?

- Now, focus on the revision. It would be better to make a revision chart for the last fifteen days before the examination. Prepare the revision schedule in such a way that the paper, which is to be held first, should come at the end of the schedule.

- You must have done the writing practice. Try to sharpen it now. Understand the importance of presentation. Keep writing continuously. Buy the stationery to be used in the examination.
- Revise the Current Affairs,including the recent ones. Now, you must not read anything new.
- In order to avoid the stress of the day just before the exam, you should plan in advance the important topics, which you wish to revise on a particular day; as it is practically impossible to revise the whole syllabus in just one day.
- Revise the notes or important sections of the Optional Subject once again.
- As the day of the Mains examination looms nearer, it is quite natural that, even after preparing well, you may feel stressed. I too was feeling stressed before the examination; but one should not lose one's confidence due to stress. I had read somewhere the following lines: "Tough time looms on everyone, Some lose confidence in it, and some win over it".
- We all know that taking unnecessary stress is not going to offer any help, instead it can harm you. If you reach the examination hall with the feeling of stress, then you may go to the extreme and fail to highlight the various relevant aspects of the question. Do not pay heed to others, especially the ones who boast and praise themselves.
- It is not necessary that only those questions, which you have not studied, will come in the examination. Therefore, think whatever you have studied is sufficient. Keep revising it, and be cool.
- Do not pay your full attention or spend more time on any one question or problem. If you do not know much about it, try to write some points and move ahead.

- Your preparation during the whole year is one aspect, and your performance in the examination hall is another aspect. Therefore, reach the examination hall happily, keeping aside each and every tension of your life.
- Besides, take care of your health yourself. Do not get confused by small things, and avoid taking stress. If anything is troubling you, think that you will handle it after the Mains examination.

What should we do in the Examination Hall?

- Do not lose your confidence during those golden three hours provided to you in the examination hall. You will not get such an opportunity quite often. Use your full energy, write for three hours, and try to solve all the questions.
- Write according to the prescribed word-limit. You must be knowing very well, how many words you write on a single page of UPSC booklet. Write only that much pages. Never waste your time counting the words in the examination hall.
- Read the questions patiently. If you do it, you will get the directions of the answer in the question itself.
- Try to increase your writing speed, but write in a legible and clear way. Underline the important points and sentences.The habit of underlining the important points leave a good impact on the examiner.
- Try to write short paragraphs.
- In a question, if it is asked to write the answer in 200 words, you can write the answer in 150-175 words. Try to write the important points and logics in the limited words only.
- While writing an answer, mention any relevant recent event, if you can recall it.

- Write the essay in paragraphs. In General Studies too, try to write in small paragraphs. If you feel it relevant to use the points in an answer, you can do so.
- If possible, try to write the answers in the same sequence in which the questions have been asked.
- Try to answer all the questions as far as possible. If you feel that you do not have enough time for writing the answer of the last few questions, in that case, do write the framework or important points of the answers.
- Try to maintain a safe distance from those 'learned' type friends, who insist on analyzing the questions and comparing its answers at the examination centre itself, just before the exam, during the lunch break or after the exam.
- If the General Studies paper or any other paper does not go well, do not take stress, as it can not improve your performance in that particular paper, but it will certainly have an adverse effect on that particular moment.
- Try to understand the various aspects of the problem in relation to one another by interconnecting them.
- Remember, a good presentation and writing your answers clearly will help you in securing good marks.
- At the end, I would say,'*All is well that ends well*'. It means, if you write your Mains examination with minimum mistakes, then all your previous mistakes will not impact your result.

❑❑

7

The Significance of Essay in Civil Services Examination

Undoubtedly, the Essay paper has a great significance in the Civil Services Examination. Though the Essay paper in this examination carries 250 marks, but it plays a significant role in achieving success in the latest pattern of the Mains examination. Ms. Ira Singhal, the topper in the Civil Services Examination, 2014, and myself, both have obtained 160 marks in the Essay paper which is probably the highest score. If you know the right strategy to write the essay, you can definitely score well in this paper, subject to your writing ability.

At the first instance, it appears that the Essay paper, just like the other seven papers, carries 250 marks,which are included in the total score (1750 marks) of the mains examination; but after analysis, we realize the significance of the marks obtained in the Essay paper. The marks, obtained by the aspirants for the last few years, suggest that a varied range of marks can be obtained in this paper. It means, you can score as low as 50 marks, or you can score even above 150 marks in this paper. This gap of 100 marks becomes very significant in your final selection and your final rank.

It is very unfortunate that the Essay paper, despite of its high significance, is neglected by the majority of the aspirants. Due to their ignorance, they neglect this paper right from the beginning of their preparations till they appear in the examination. There are many who never practice the writing of essays and they write their first essay in the examination hall only ! They are of the view that spending time on the preparation of Essay paper is useless, as this paper is very subjective in nature, and there is no fixed formula for its preparation.

In my opinion, the neglect of the Essay paper in the preparations for the Civil Services examination is not advisable at all, as this paper does play a pivotal role in the final selection and in getting a good rank too. Having realized its great significance, I devised a strategy in my overall process of preparations, and gave a priority to the preparation of the Essay paper. Fortunately, I got the benefits of it.

No doubt, the Essay paper is subjective, there is no fixed formula for its preparations,and no one can predict the marks one hopes to obtain in this paper. Nevertheless, there are some methods and techniques also, which can help you in performing well, as well as assure you of getting at least more than the average marks. I firmly believe that a definite strategy for its proper preparation and a full dedication will enable you to perform excellently in this extremely important paper. I will discuss some useful methods and strategies for performing well in the Essay paper to make the preparation of this paper more objective and easy.

In this chapter, I will discuss some important aspects related to the Essay paper; then I will try to clarify the various doubts the aspirants have about this paper. First of all, you should understand the expectations of the Union Public Service Commission from the aspirants appearing in this paper. The UPSC syllabus states, "*Candidates may be required to write essays on multiple topices. They will be expected to keep closely to the subject of the essay to arrange their ideas in orderly fashion and to write concisely. Credit will be given to effective and exact expression*".

Let us understand the syllabus of Essay paper prescribed for the Civil Services examination.We find in it that the emphasis is on the following four points:

1. To remain completely focused on the topic.
2. To express the views in an organized manner.
3. To write in brief but comprehensively.
4. To present an error-free, meticulous and effective expression.

There can be many more points regarding the preparation of the Essay paper, but here, I would discuss the above four more important points:

1. **To remain completely focused on the topic:** The best mantra for the essay writing is to remain connected to the basic idea of the topic. Throughout, the inclination of the whole essay should be towards the topic. The examiner must not feel that you have deviated from the topic. Though, a common topic is generally kept in the Essay paper, but sometimes, it is abstract in nature. If you cover the positive as well as the negative aspects of that topic,and present your ideas in an organized manner, then it will not be difficult to fetch good marks.
2. **To express your views in an organized manner:** In fact, an essay reflects not only the writing style of its writer, but it presents the writer's knowledge, experience and thought process also. Thus, if our expression in the essay is disorganized and confusing, it lowers the quality of our essay. I have seen that many aspirants, though they are rich in ideas, but while writing an essay they fail to express their ideas in an orderly, organized and well planned manner.Therefore, you should refrain from the tendency of organizing the 'mismatched ideas'. It is better to make a brief framework to express your ideas in a well planned manner and include the various aspects of the topic in this framework, substantiating each aspect with the relevant example, utterances, quotes etc.

3. **To write in brief but comprehensively:** Write to the point, but comprehensively and effectively. Keep in mind, *'Excess of everything is bad'*. Remember, you are supposed to write two essays within the limited time frame of three hours, therefore avoid crossing the word limit. Write in paragraphs, but avoid writing long paragraphs. 'Expressing more ideas in less words' is an art, and writing briefly is useful not only for the essay writing, but also for the other mediums of expression, like debate, speech, interview, discussion and lecture etc.
4. **To present an error-free, meticulous and effective expression:** Expression is the most important quality of a good essay. We will discuss it in detail. However, if you keep the above points in your mind and follow them while writing your essay, then your essay will definitely become accurate and effective.

To meet the above four-point criteria for writing the Essay paper, you must keep in mind the following points:

1. **Flow:** The most attractive feature of the essay writing is its 'flow'. If there is a spontaneous flow in the essay, the examiner's interest in the essay will be maintained from the beginning till the end, which will definitely help you in getting good marks. Now, the question is, 'how to maintain the flow while writing an essay'. Remember, essay is an organized, well planned and sequential presentation of ideas. Therefore, while presenting your ideas, identify the interrelated ideas, and present these interrelated ideas sequentially in your essay, e.g., when you complete one paragraph and start writing another paragraph, link the

beginning of the second paragraph with the end of the first paragraph. There must be a connection between the two paragraphs. In an essay, such a flow can be developed with a regular practice.

2. **Balanced view/middle path:** Though the thoughts and views of the aspirants and the examiners are different, but both can be correct. Therefore, instead of choosing the extreme path, it is better to take a middle path while writing an essay. Buddha's philosophy of 'Middle path' can be very beneficial while writing an essay.
3. **Comprehensive views covering all the aspects:** If your narrative is good and broad, your expression can be effective and accurate. Avoid the narrow ideas and use a balanced view, viewing everything in its totality. For this, it is necessary to identify the various interrelated aspects inherent in the topic, and discuss them in a well organized manner. In the present academic world, it is an age of the inter-disciplinary studies, where the various faculties/subjects/disciplines of learning are interrelated. It is similar to the syllabus of General Studies in which all the sections are interrelated with one another. After analyzing the interrelation among the various dimensions of learning and its power to influence one another, we find that in reality, an essay is '*the well planned and organized development of a specific topic which covers all its relevant aspects*'.

To understand the various aspects of the essay and to develop it in an organized manner, the limits of essay's topic need to be extended. Some of the probable aspects (not compulsory) can be as follows:

1. Social
2. Cultural/literary
3. Economic
4. Political/Administration/Managerial
5. Philosophical

6. Religious/Spiritual
7. Scientific/Technical
8. Historical
9. Geographical
10. Diplomatic
11. Demographic
12. Environmental/Ecological
13. Gender- based differences

By keeping the above list in your mind, you can develop the various aspects of the topic in an organized manner. In addition, you must keep in mind the following points also:

(i) Try to understand all the aspects of the various problems. Our administrative and political structure starts from the villages/towns and crosses through the districts, states; and then it spreads across the country and the world. Therefore, look at the problems from all the angles.

(ii) Doing activities for the welfare of the deprived classes is the main responsibility of 'a welfare state'. As an alert and responsible citizen, it is our moral duty to be sensitive towards their sufferings. By taking the marginalized or the deprived classes together, we can achieve the target of 'inclusive development'.

The list of marginalized or deprived classes can be as follows:

1. Scheduled caste/tribe; (SC/ST)
2. Other backward classes; (OBC)
3. Minorities;
4. Differently-abled persons;
5. Women and children;
6. Senior citizens;
7. Marginal farmers and laborers of the unorganized sector;
8. Third gender.

(iii) Further, there can be some more aspects of development as given below:

1. Education, 2. Health, 3. Employment,
4. Agriculture, 5. Rural development,
6. Poverty eradication, 7. Sanitation,
8. Justice, 9. Energy,
10. Environment and Bio-diversity conservation,
11. Communication and transportation etc.

4. **Totality and respecting other's view:** Try to look at the things in its totality. The learning is multidimensional. Just focusing on one aspect of anything, and ignoring its other aspects, is not logical. Remember the example of the seven blind persons, who try to understand an elephant by touching its seven different parts of body. They find that the elephant is not a tail or a trunk only, it is a complete entity in itself.
   Similarly, do not consider only your own idea as the best. Respect the views of others,as per 'Anekantavad' and 'Syaydvad', the principles of Jainism. Respecting the view of everyone and perceiving the subject in its totality can make your essay extensive, balanced and multi-dimensional.
5. **Introduction and conclusion:** Most of the aspirants get confused about the way of writing the introduction and conclusion of an essay. In fact, there is no fixed formula for writing the introduction and conclusion. The introduction of an essay should be original. There are different techniques for it,e.g., some begin the introduction with a saying/ quotation, some with a story, some with the topic's background, while some with the topic's basic facts. You can select any one of these techniques, or you can use some other technique. Just make sure that your introduction is visionary and effective.
   After writing the introduction, develop the essay's topic and try to maintain a flow. Do not forget to

write the conclusion in the end. There can be many ways of writing a conclusion, but try to avoid an extreme view or a pessimistic conclusion. Present a balanced, tactful, positive and optimistic opinion in the conclusion. It is unlikely that you will get the benefit of using an extreme sentimentality or outrageousness.

6. **Writing style and presentation:** We observe that ' the taste of the food' and ' the way it has been served' are two completely different things. If the food is tasty and it is served in a nice way also, it looks like an icing on the cake. In the same way, if your ideas, facts and logics are good and effective, and your presentation of those ideas is also done in an effective manner, it will impress the examiner for sure. The Commission's guidelines do not clarify about the presentation style,though, it emphasizes on a 'legible hand-writing'.In my view, if you keep the following points in mind, you can improve your style of presenting the ideas:
   (i) Write in short paragraphs. Writing two to three paragraphs in one page of the answer-sheet leaves a good impression on the examiner.
   (ii) The grammatical errors or the spelling mistakes leave a negative impact on the examiner. Therefore, try to avoid these linguistic errors.
   (iii) The grammatical purity does not mean 'use of a pure language'. It means that you should use the simple words. You can use the technical terms/terminology also, if it is required in the context. You must always keep in mind that the language used by you should not be mechanical or artificial, instead it should be simple and spontaneous.

(iv) Many aspirants worry about their hand-writing. No doubt,a good hand writing beautifies your presentation, and leaves a positive effect on the examiner's mind. Thus, write neatly and clearly. A Readability should be maintained, so that the examiner does not face any difficulty in reading the essay.

(v) You can underline the important points to highlight them.

7. **Use of dictums/statements/citations/quotations:** Sometimes, the aspirants ask questions, like 'Whether one should use the dictums/statements/citations or not, and 'which one of them should be used'. I feel, if the sayings or dictums of the learned persons/thinkers/philosophers are relevant to the topic, they can be used without hesitation, but try to note down them while preparing the essay's framework itself.

   Remember, theuse the dictums should be according to the context and in a natural manner. It should not appear as if it is being imposed; rather it should suit the essay's topic. Try to maintain a flow.Avoid quoting the controversial statements.

8. **Use of qualitative content:** There is a saying, 'the more sugar you use, the sweeter a dish becomes'. Therefore, a good and qualitative material always helps in improving the quality of your essay. Remember, never let the ideological narrowness or superficiality be reflected in your essay. For instance:

   (a) The ideas expressed in your writing should not reflect any casteism, regionalism, communalism or any language-bias.

   (b) Although the philosophy of life and statements of many thinkers/ personalities, like Aristotle, Socrates, Plato, Buddha, Mahavir, Guru Nanak, Kabir, Raidas, Tulsi, Gandhi, Nehru,

Tagore, Ambedkar, Vivekananda, Aurobindo etc. can be quoted, but never limit yourself to a specific religion, philosophy or spiritualism; instead use the quotations of the best Indian and Western scholars in history, language, literature, psychology, political science, sociology, science, technology, management, law, administration etc., as per the need of the context.

The values and ideals of Indian Freedom Movement and the philosophy of Indian Constitution are our guide and inspiration. According to the context in your essay, you can take the references from the preamble of the Constitution of India, the fundamental duties, directive principles of the state-policy and the fundamental rights.

(c) It is better to take a help of the facts and figures, wherever they are required for validating your views; but it should be done without affecting the flow of the essay.

(d) Merely criticizing the government's policies can not be the solution of any problem. There is a story in this context, as given below:

'Once upon a time a painter painted a picture and hung it at a railway station platform. He wrote that please mark the mistakes in the picture. The next day when he reached the station, he found that the whole picture was marked with the signs. The painter painted a second picture. He hung the second picture at the same place. Now, he wrote that please correct the mistakes you find in this picture. The next day, when we went to see the picture, he was astonished to see that the picture was left unmarked'.

The moral of this story is that it is easy to pose a problem, but it is very difficult to offer a solution to that problem.

There is a famous statement by Shiv Khera, a motivational speaker, "*If we are not a part of the solution, then we are the problem in ourselves*".

Hence, avoid the tendency of complaining; instead accept the welfare schemes and programmes with a positive attitude. In my opinion, any state makes these welfare schemes and programmes for the betterment of its citizens.

9. **Selection of the topic:** You can win half of the battle, if you select the right topic for the essay. There is a proverb, '*Well begun is half done*'. If you select a right topic, then the probability of writing a good essay increases. Therefore, while selecting the topic of an essay, try to keep the following points in mind:
   (a) Select a topic which you are most familiar with. For example in my exam, I selected the topic, 'Is sting operation an invasion on privacy', because I had a reasonably good understanding of this topic. In the same way, you can select your topic from the field of literature/ philosophy/geography/science/ culture, if you have a better understanding of any one of them.
   (b) Give the first preference to those topics in which you possess enough material, and you have logics to validate your statements. Not only this, you should be confident also that you can write a good essay on this topic. You are lucky, if some topics in the exam are similar to the topics you have prepared during the essay writing practice. I would suggest that you should prefer such topics.

10. **What to do and what not:** You must never neglect the essay paper, and study certain things in a general way. At the preparation and strategy level, you should understand the following things also which can assure a better performance in the essay paper:
    (i) The habit of studying and then thinking over it, makes your ideas more mature. It also increases your thinking power.
    Do develop and maintain the habit of reading, writing, discussing and thinking.Do not limit the sources of knowledge; keep reading good books and magazines and learning new things.
    (ii) There is no other substitute for the writing practice.If you want to perfect it, practice the writing of essays every week; and. get them evaluated so that you can improve your writing skill.
    (iii) The Group Discussion is a dynamic and participatory way of doing the preparations which makes our ideas rich and long lasting. Even the Upanishad confirms it:
    'Vad-vivadaah jaayte tatvabodhah'.
    (You get elemental knowledge from the discussions)
    (iv) Knowledge is infinite like an ocean. Remember, we taste only a few drops of this ocean. Therefore, never behave like an 'empty vessel'which makes much noise, and never let your ego come in the process of learning. Socrates, the great philosopher, says, *"The only true wisdom is in knowing you know nothing"*.
    (v) Have full faith in yourself and your preparations and thoughts, instead of having over confidence. If you practice the writing

of essays continuously, the quality of your essays will improve gradually. Then, you will be able to write a better essay in the examination.

(vi) Give a special attention to the time-division. It is compulsory to write both the essays in the paper. So, devote equal time to them. It does not matter,if you give more 5 - 10 minutes more to the first essay. Try to write the essays in the same sequence in which they have been asked in the paper.

(vii) Do not cross the word limit, as you will not get any credit for it.

(viii) Lastly, try to maintain the positive energy. You should not lose your hope at any cost, neither during the preparations nor in the examination hall.

Always remember the following lines of Dushyant Kumar, the Hindi poet:

"Who says that a hole cannot be done in the sky?
Just throw a stone with full enthusiasm at the sky".

Some More Useful Tips

1. There is no other substitute for the writing practice. Therefore, sit for three- hours every week, and practice the writing of two full essays within one and a half hour. It will be very beneficial for you.
2. In the first few minutes, make a written framework of the essay. You can include the relevant aspects, facts, examples and utterances to expand the essay's topic.
3. Take some time to select the topic. You should always select the topic from the field in which you have full grasp and understanding. For example, the aspirants from the science background can write comparatively a better essay on the technical topics. I chose the topic of essays from literature,

culture, mass communication and philosophy, because I had more interest and understanding in these subjects. Thus, my advice is that you should decide your topic on the basis of your interest and understanding of the subject.

4. Begin your essay by writing a preface. The preface can have some famous statements or quotations and some examples or the background of the topic; but it should have a vision, and should hint at the topic's expansion.
5. Write the essay in paragraphs. It looks nice if a page contains at least two or three paragraphs.
6. While developing the topic, try to discuss the untouched aspects of that topic,like economic, social, cultural, philosophical, historical and scientific etc. The more aspects your essay covers, the more effective it will be; but should avoid an unnecessary expansion.
7. Write in a sequential and organized manner. Writing haphazardly leaves a negative impact on the examiner.
8. Do not waste your time and efforts by crossing the word limit.
9. Remember, your essay will reflect the gist of your study and experience, gained in your life.

Useful Tables for Essay

For your convenience, I am sharing with you some tables of facts and information, which can be used to develop the essay's content according to their relevance. By using these tables, you can make your essay more extensive, compendious and inclusive:

Table 1: Level of development

1. Person/Individual
2. Family
3. Society

4. Village
5. Town
6. City
7. State
8. Nation
9. World

Table 2: Some targeted classes for social welfare

1. Scheduled Caste(SC)
2. Scheduled Tribes (ST)
3. Other Backward Class(OBC)
4. Minority
5. Women
6. Children
7. Senior citizen
8. Physically handicapped/differently abled persons
9. Third gender/LGBT
10. Marginal farmer
11. People below poverty line [BPL]
12. Street vendor
13. Laborers of the unorganized sector

Table 3: Various philosophies/discourses

1. Gandhism
2. Marxism
3. Communism
4. Capitalism
5. Socialism
6. Liberalism
7. Existentialism
8. Humanism
9. Utilitarianism
10. Women discourse
11. Dalit discourse
12. Tribal discourse

Table 4: Major philosophies of the nation builders of India

1. Mahatama Gandhi-Non-Violence, truth, trusteeship, Satyagraha, Sarvodaya;
2. Jawaharlal Nehru-Socialism, secularism, democracy;
3. Rabindranath Tagore-Internationalism, humanism, nationalism, renaissance, modernism;
4. Dr. Bhimrao Ambedkar- Social justice, affirmative action, human rights;
5. Swami Vivekananda- Spiritualism, tolerance, neo Vedanta.

Table 5: Major challenges before India

1. Casteism
2. Regionalism
3. Language-bias
4. Communalism
5. Criminalization
6. Climate change
7. Poverty
8. Inequality
9. Racism/extremism
10. Terrorism

Table 6: Our important rights

1. Right to Information
2. Right to Education
3. Right to Food Security
4. Right to Privacy
5. Right to Rehabilitation and Resettlement
6. Right to Social Security
7. Right to Rural Employment Guarantee
8. Forest Rights

Table 7: The foundation of our Constitutional values

1. Preamble of the constitution
2. Fundamental rights
3. Fundamental duties
4. Directive Principles of the state policy

Table 8: Our universal values

1. Equality
2. Freedom
3. Fraternity
4. Non-Violence
5. Equity
6. Tolerance
7. Secularism
8. Socialism
9. Integration

❑❑

8

Optional Subject: The Game Changer

After the year 2013, the pattern of Civil Services Examination has been changed substantially. Now, the aspirants have to choose just one optional subject, instead of two optional subjects. Now the proverb 'Jack of all trades, master of none' may be modified as: 'Jack of all trades, master of one' to suit the new pattern.

Why Optional Subject is so Important?

Although the marks secured in the optional subject and its impact on the marks sheet has reduced, and the Mains exam of Civil Services is now comprised of just one optional subject, but the optional subject still remains the key factor to secure a good rank in this examination. If you look at the mark sheets of the UPSC toppers of the last four to five years, you will realize that the marks obtained in the optional subject by the UPSC toppers are extraordinary and much higher than those of the other aspirants.

For instance in their respective optional subjects, all the toppers had scored more than 250 marks out of the total 500 marks, e.g., Gaurav Agrawal, the topper in the Civil Services Examination, 2013, obtained 296, in Economics; Ira Singhal, the topper in 2014, obtained 305 marks in Geography; I (Nishant Jain) obtained 313 marks in Hindi Literature; Tina Dabi, the topper in 2015, obtained 299 marks in Political Science. Nandini KR, the topper of Civil Services Exam, 2016 obtained 331 marks in Kannada Literature. It clearly suggests that the optional subject holds an important place in this examination and plays a pivotal role in the making of the UPSC toppers.

The Optional subject is important for the aspirants for some other reasons too. Firstly, the optional subject's syllabus is relatively fixed. Generally in it, the questions are asked from within the syllabus; and in this paper, you can remain more confident than in the General Studies paper. Though the syllabus of General Studies is fixed too, but the nature of General Studies is such that it is very difficult to limit its broad areas in a defined syllabus. In this way, by preparing and revising well the defined syllabus of the optional subject,you can obtain good marks in this paper.

Secondly, the mark sheets of the successful candidates indicate that the range of marks obtained by them varies, i.e., some score less than 200 marks, while some score more than 300 marks.However, the range of marks in the General Studies paper does not vary much.

How to Select the Optional Subject?

There is a saying,'Well begun is half done'. Thus, selecting the right optional subject is very important for any aspirant. If you select the right optional subject, then you can begin your preparations for the Civil Services examination in a better way and can get a much better outcome.

I have seen many aspirants changing their optional subjects many times. Therefore, think twice before selecting the optional subject, so that you need not change your decision frequently.

First of all you must know that, as per UPSC rules, it is not obligatory to have studied the chosen optional subject as one of the subjects at your graduation or post-graduation level. It means, that in spite of having a B.Tech degree in the Computer Science, you can choose the History or Philosophy subject as your optional subject for the Mains exam, subject to the condition that the chosen optional subject should be from the list of the subjects prescribed in the syllabus of the Civil services examination.

The list of optional subjects is as follows:

- Agriculture
- Animal Husbandry and Veterinary Science
- Anthropology
- Botany
- Chemistry
- Civil Engineering
- Commerce and Accountancy
- Economics
- Electrical Engineering
- Geography
- Geology
- History
- Law
- History
- Management
- Mathematics
- Mechanical Engineering
- Medical Sciences
- Philosophy
- Physics
- Political Science and International Relations
- Psychology
- Public Administration
- Statistics
- Zoology
- Literature of any one of the 22 Indian languages mentioned in the Eighth Schedule of the Constitution of India, and English Literature.

While selecting the optional subject, you must keep the following points in your mind:

1. While selecting the optional subject, it is compulsory for you to know whether you have some interest in that subject or not, and whether you feel enthusiasm and interest or not, while studying that subject. It is important, because the syllabus of the Optional Subject in the Civil

Services examination is broad, and without having an interest and zeal in the particular subject, it becomes very difficult to do its preparations. Your interest and enthusiasm will help you in avoiding the boredom, which crops up in the process of doing the optional subject preparations.

2. Besides, you must also analyze whether you have familiarity with that subject or not. At times, you select the subject from your educational background which you are more familiar with and have more command. For example, I did my M.A. and M.Phil. in Hindi Literature, and selected the same subject as my optional subject. Now-a-days, this trend is very popular. Especially the graduates and post-graduates in the Medical sciences, Law, Management, Commerce, Science and Engineering, they select the optional subjects from their study background. You should not select the optional subject blindly from the subjects of your study background, unless it is a scoring and well performing subject in the Civil Services examination.
3. It is important to analyze the trend of that subject; and whether that subject is fetching good marks or not in the last two or three years.
4. However, you must not select any subject only on this basis that it will help in other papers of the mains exam, like General Studies, Essay or Ethics. Your first and foremost focus should be on selecting an optional subject which can help you in scoring the maximum marks.
5. You must consider the other factors too while choosing your Optional subject, like whether a good and authentic material of the selected optional subject is available in your language medium, or whether the guidance is available, when you need it.

If you keep the above points in mind, you will be able to choose the most suitable optional subject. It is always better to think yourself or take the advice from some experienced person, before selecting an optional subject. There is a proverb, 'Indecision is often worse than the wrong decision'. Therefore, avoid the state of indecision, as it will lead to the wastage of your attempts; and choose a suitable optional subject on the basis of its merit.

How to Prepare the Optional Subject?

The syllabus of the Optional subject in the Civil Services examination is very detailed. It is comprised of two papers of 250 marks each. Generally, the first paper is more theoretical and the second paper is more practical and applied.

You should keep the following points in mind while preparing for your Optional subject:

1. Firstly, go through the papers of the last five years. Try to understand the objective of the Civil Services examination for this paper. You must understand the difference between this paper and the regular university papers.
2. Take guidance, if you are selecting an optional subject not related to your educational background.You can take help from the relevant books on the subject chosen by you or even from your experienced teachers, while doing its preparations.
3. You must cover the whole syllabus prescribed for the optional subject.
4. Making notes and revising them from time to time is a must. Besides this, you should practice the answer-writing also. You must not forget to get your answers evaluated by your seniors or by your experienced teachers. Joining a good Test Series is also a good option.
5. Remember,while preparing for the Civil Services Examination, you should not study the Optional subject in the manner you study while researching

on a topic/subject for the M.Phil/Ph.D. degree. Your preparations for this subject should be of the graduation (Honours.) instead.

6. If you happen to meet another aspirant, who is also preparing for the same optional subject, then have the subject- related discussions with him/her. It may be beneficial for you.

❑❑

9

How to Prepare the Current Affairs?

The Current Affairs has been important in the Civil Services Examinations conducted by UPSC and State Public Service Commissions, and remains unchanged even in its latest pattern. In all the three stages of the Civil Services Examination,i.e., prelims exam, mains exam and interview, it is essential to have a deep understanding of the Current Affairs, its background and impact on the socio-economic life of our nation and the world for performing well and succeeding in the Examination.

For the last few years, not many questions were asked from the Current Affairs in the Preliminary examination; but in the Preliminary Examination, Civil Services, 2016, the Current Affairs comprised a major portion of the first paper. Therefore, it is very necessary to cover the Current Affairs fully and acquire an accuracy for clearing the Preliminary examination. For example, if you have the correct and full knowledge of the main components of the new public welfare schemes, initiated by Government of India, or you have a general understanding of the features of developments in the field of science and technology, you will be able to solve the multiple choice questions and identify the right and wrong options as well.

Look at the following examples:

Question: 'Rashtriya Garima Abhiyaan' is a national campaign to

(a) Rehabilitate the homeless and destitute persons and provide them with suitable sources of livelihood.

(b) Release the sex workers from thair practice and provide them with alternative sources of livelihood.
(c) Eradicate the practice of manual scavenging and rehabilitate the manual scarvengers.
(d) Release the bonded labourers from their bondage and rehabilitate them.

Such questions from the Current Affairs, asked in the Preliminary examination, are comparatively easy. If you study the newspapers and magazines seriously for the whole year, you can easily identify that this mission is related to the practice of manual scavenging.

Question: The establishment of 'Payment Banks' is being allowed in India to promote financial inclusion. Which of the following statements is/are correct in this context?

1. Mobile telephone companies and supermarket chains that are owned and controlled by residents are eligible to be promoters of Payment Banks.
2. Payment Banks can issue both credit cards and debit cards.
3. Payment Banks cannot undertake lending activities.

Select the correct answer using the code given below:

(a) 1 and 2 only
(b) 1 and 3 only
(c) 2 only
(d) 1, 2 and 3

Such types of questions demand sharp eyes and an accurate knowledge. For answering the above question, you must have the knowledge of the important features and objectives of the Payment Banks.

Every year, many questions related to the Current Affairs are asked in the Civil Services Mains Examination directly or indirectly. For preparing this paper, knowing the essence of any event, i.e., its causes and effects, is more important than knowing merely the facts. Any event, happening at the national and international level, does not happen suddenly. Some of its causes remain hidden in the past or in the present and they have a deep impact on the nation, society and the international relations. The Mains examination demands this kind of reading and understanding of the Current Affairs. In my understanding, an aspirant should prepare at least five to six major points related to any event, in order to deal with the Current Affairs in the Mains examination. The Current Affairs of a year, before the Mains exams and till one month prior to the Mains exam, is more relevant from the point of view of examination.

The following are some more examples :

Question: How can the 'Digital India' programme help farmers to improve productivity and income? What step has the government taken in this regard?

Question: The human rights activists constantly highlight the fact that Armed Forces (Special Powers) Act, 1958, is a draconian act; leading to the cases of human rights abuses by the Armed Forces. What Sections of the Act are opposed by the activists? Critically evaluate the requirement with the reference to the view held by the Apex Court.

Both the questions mentioned above are related to the Current Affairs. The first question is comparatively easy. In writing its answer, you can tell about the efforts made by the government, and can discuss the effects of this programme on agriculture; but the second question demands a deep idea and knowledge of the Current Affairs as well as your own ideas and views on the Armed Forces (Special Powers) Act, 1958. You can answer this question if you have studied and comprehended the recent debates and the views of the court on this act.

About fifty percent of the questions asked in the personality test or interview are related to Current Affairs. The main reason behind this is that the Interview Board wants to know your views and opinions on the various issues and problems in order to test your personality. For this, the board takes the help of the recent events taking place at the national and international level. The events can be related to your state, country, neighbouring countries and to the world. There are various ways to ask the answer to these questions.Sometimes the questions having one word answer are asked, e.g.,'Who has been awarded with this year's Nobel Prize and why'? Generally in the interview, the questions are asked to know your clear view on various current issues,e.g.,'Why India felt the need to do a surgical strike on the Line of Control, or Should India have done so'?

Generally, very old questions related to the Current Affairs are not asked in the interview.Mostly the questions, which are about three-four months old from the date of interview, are asked in the interview. Hence, you can easily prepare the Current Affairs for the interview after appearing in the mains examination.

Since the importance of Current Affairs in the Civil Services examination has increased manifold now, let us discuss how to do an overall and effective preparation for it. In my view, some of the important ways of doing its preparations are as follows:

Reading Newspapers

Everyone suggests that one should read a good and standard newspaper; but the questions is which newspaper one should read, and how to read a newspaper.The major newspapers of English are, 'The Hindu' and 'The Indian Express'. Out of the two, 'The Hindu' is more popular among the UPSC aspirants.

Now the question is how to read a newspaper. You should prefer the paper which you can read and comprehend well. My suggestion is that you should never read too many newspapers. It is sufficient to read one or two newspapers. You must read the front page, national and international news page, sports page, science and technology and arts-culture page of the newspaper. Besides, you can underline the important points while reading it, and can also make the notes by noting these points in a diary or a register. While reading a newspaper, some aspirants underline the important news of the newspaper, cut that news or graphics and keep it in their files. For doing so, it is better to compile the cuttings of the different sections of the General Studies separately, like polity, economy, society, international issues and science-technology. Besides, you should read a good monthly magazine to know the issues and the background behind that particular news.

Most of the aspirants complain that reading a newspaper consumes much time. In this regard I would say that, if you continue the habit of reading a newspaper, you will gradually start understanding which news should be given importance and which news is to be avoided. In any case, you must not devote more than one and a half hour or maximum two hours in total to read a newspaper.

Role of Magazines

For the preparations of the Civil Services examination, various good competitive magazines are available, like Civil Services Times, EPW, Frontline, Chronicle etc. They are good because they present an analysis of all the current events and changes happened during the last month, along with their background, important factors and effects. In my view, you should include at least one competitive magazine in your preparations, as it helps in the detailed revision of the things which you have studied in the newspaper the last month.

Besides, the two magazines,'Yojana' and 'Kurukshetra', published by the Government of India, are extremely important. Both of them are published in the various Indian Languages, including Hindi and English. You will not require much time to study these monthly magazines, but they will develop your understanding of the various government welfare schemes and initiatives as well as the rural development scenario. Out of these two magazines, I would recommend for the 'Yojana' more, as every issue of the 'Yojana' is generally focused on some important subject areas.

Besides this, the Publications Division, Government of India, issues an annual reference book, which is known as the 'India Year Book'. It is published in both the Hindi and English languages. It contains the general introduction of various ministries and departments of Government of India and their achievements during the last year. You must Study it, as it is quite useful.

It is not advised to read the above magazines page by page. You may study only those topics in these magazines, which you find useful for you from the examination point of view.

Internet and Social Media

In the age of information revolution, I suggest you to use the internet for the academic and creative purpose. You can find very important current affairs related information on many government and non-government websites. The information given on these websites proves to be very useful from the point of view of the Civil Services Examination. Some of the important websites are as follows:
india.gov.in, newsonair.com, pib.nic.in, mrunal.org, insightsonindia.com, unacademy.in, myGov.in, PRSindia.org, and the websites of various ministries.

You need not visit these websites daily or spend most of your time on the internet. Use internet creatively, along with time management. The same is applicable to the use of social media, like Facebook, twitter etc. Talking about myself, I used the social media in order to read the posts of renowned writers or to study good articles. It has helped me not only in developing the new ideas, but also in developing the writing skill.

Radio/T.V.

We should use the radio and T.V to make our learning effective. The teachers also use the audio-visual aids to make their teaching effective. For instance, listen to the All India Radio news analysis, while walking in the evening; listen to the debates on current issues on D.D.News, Rajya Sabha T.V., and Lok Sabha T.V.It will broaden your thoughts by increasing the limits of your thinking.

In the leisurely time, you can watch the episodes of the T.V serials, like 'Yes Minister', 'Satyamev Jayate', 'Pradhanmantri', 'Samvidhan', and 'Bharat Ek Khoj'.

Link your Basic Knowledge with Current Affairs

Linking the current affairs with the basic General Studies is an art. Understand this art, as it is very necessary for the preparations of the Civil Services examination. Understanding the art of linking the current affairs with the basic General Studies can make your answers special, better than others. You must not see any event from a narrow view, you should see the events in their totality instead. If you understand the background and the impact of every event, you will be able to link it with the basic information given in the General Studies. For instance, while discussing various topics like citizen charter, Panchayati Raj or All India Services, you must possess the basic related provisions mentioned in the constitution or in the law. In this way, the knowledge of Current Affairs will update your knowledge of General Studies too.

Keep your Eyes and Ears Open

Union Public Service Commission expects from the aspirants that they must be aware of their surroundings. For this, it is essential to be aware of your socio-cultural-economic-political environment. Never ignore the advertisements, related to the Government Welfare Schemes, which are published in the newspapers. I used to read the health awareness related advertisements of the government, while travelling in the Delhi Metro. I mean to say that you should make a good use of the time to learn many new things.

Relevance of Group Discussion

For the preparations of the Current Affairs, a positive discussion in the group proves to be very useful. It is a fact

that we tend to forget some points after reading them, but we do remember the same if we hear those points repeatedly, and share them with others in the group discussion. Another important benefit of group discussion is that you come to know the contrary views and logics on the various issues. It helps in forming your own view. If you are able to form your own view through the group discussions, it will help you a lot in the interview.
The following proverb in English endorses the usefulness of group discussion:

"Tell me and I forget,
Teach me and I remember,
Involve me and I learn".

Remember,your group should not be very large; and the fellow aspirants, taking part in the discussion, should be focused towards the preparations of examination.

❑❑

10 Significance of Having Command over Your Language

"Words are pale shadows of forgotten names. As names have power, words have power. Words can light fires in the minds of men. Words can wring tears from the hardest hearts".

–Patrick Rothfuss

The above quotation makes you realize the power of the language. The words can express your views in an effective manner. A command over your language medium provides an expression to your creativity, words to your imagination and shape to your statements. It helps you in performing well in every walks of life, and it is very much relevant in the context of the Civil Services examination.

I have experienced that the following qualities in the toppers of the Civil Services examination have made the path of their success much easier, and also made them different from others:

(i) Effective command over language,
(ii) Excellent writing skill,
(iii) Broad view,
(iv) Broad area of knowledge.

It does not matter which language you choose as the medium, but a good command over that language medium will make your path to success easier. The four qualities mentioned above are, more or less, related to the command over the language. Thus, having a good command over your language will improve not only your writing skill, but also your reading skill.Your habit of reading the good books will make your view complete and comprehensive, enable you to understand and connect to the things in a better way and will increase your knowledge and understanding as well.

In order to perfect your language, you should practise the following four skills:

- Listening skill
- Speaking skill
- Reading skill
- Writing skill

Mastering these four language skills will give you a command over your language. Francis Bacon, in his famous essay, 'Of Studies', writes that:

"Reading makes a full man;
Conference a ready man;
Writing an Exact man,
Reading adds perfection to a man's personality".

Though the listening skill is a very important skill, but it is often ignored, considering it as an unnecessary skill. In the context of the preparations for Civil Services examination, it has been observed that those aspirants, who listen to the various lectures in the class, videos, T.V. show, radio etc. patiently, understand the concepts better and acquire substantial knowledge. Hence, developing the listening skill is equally important as the skills of reading and writing are in the Civil Services Examination,. For this purpose, it is necessary that one must develop the habit of listening patiently, concentrating one's mind on that thing. The habit of listening patiently, understanding it and then responding to it helps not only during the studies but also in the interview.

The speaking skill is the second most important skill in the language learning process. Like the other skills,this skill cannot be developed in a day; it is developed with a continuous practice instead. The signs of a good speaking skill are: speaking clearly, pronouncing correctly, having flow, selecting the words according to the context, taking necessary pauses, emphasizing on the important points and speaking with intonation. Mastering this skill proves very useful in the interview, which can affect the examination's result to a great extent. Remember, only a good reader can become a good writer and similarly, only a good listener can become a good speaker.

Let us discuss the two skills,i.e., reading and writing, which are very important from the point of view of the Civil Services Examination. Developing the reading and writing skills is essential as per the requirements of the Preliminary and Mains examination. Taking the reading skill very lightly, the aspirants sometimes ignore it, but you must keep in mind that the reading skill plays a pivotal role in both the papers of the Preliminary examination as well as in all the nine papers of the Mains examination. You need to develop the reading and comprehension skills in order to read and comprehend more in less time, and perform well in the comprehension section of C-SAT (second paper). Developing your reading and comprehension skills will help you in getting a command over your language and in understanding the questions of the first paper.

The command over reading and writing skills can improve your performance to a great extent in all the nine papers, i.e., the papers of Essay and Ethics, Optional Subject, General Studies Paper I, II and III, along with the two compulsory language papers (Hindi and English) of the Mains examination. If you have a good command over your language, you will have the following benefits:

1. Can understand the right context of the language;
2. Can give the relevant answers by correctly comprehending the meaning of the key words in the subjects of Ethics, polity and economy.
3. It is necessary to understand the registers of a language. The style of a language differs in different areas and in different contexts,e.g., the register of market, the register of cinema, the register of literature, the resister of the academic

world, the register of the government offices etc. You must comprehend the registers of your language medium and the contexts in which these registers are used. Try to speak and write accordingly.

4. If you are good at reading and writing, your speed of reading and writing will also be increased. It is observed that the aspirants, who read and write fast, certainly perform better than the other aspirants. Remember, your writing speed will play an important role in the General Studies.

Sometimes, the aspirants do not have the habit of reading some good and new books and magazines, as they do not realize the importance of sparing some of their time for reading the fiction or non-fiction.You must keep in mind that it is necessary to form a general reading habit, as reading the good books and magazines enhances your understanding, broadens your view and strengthens your command over your language.

A command over the language and its vocabulary enables you to comprehend better and express your ideas more interestingly and effectively, i.e., you can beautify your expressions by making a relevant use of the right words, idioms, proverbs or the poetic lines at the right moment; you can comprehend well the complicated and tough language of the question paper, and can write the comprehensive answers accordingly. Hence, if you want to achieve a good rank in the Civil Services examination, you must not ignore the four language skills, and must work hard on developing these language skills. Ludwig Wittgenstein, a philosopher, highlights the significance of the language skills in the following manner:

"The limits of my language mean the limits of my world".

❑❑

11

Writing Skill: The Basis of Success

The process of self development goes on continuously,i.e., daily we learn something new by listening, speaking, reading and writing, then we incorporate them in our overall personality. These four things together shape our personality on a daily basis, and as a result, we make a qualitative improvement in ourselves and move ahead on the path of success.

In this chapter, we will do a special discussion on the 'Writing skill', which is the most important skill among the four language skills. We will also try to know how can you improve your writing skill qualitatively. In the current scenario of the Civil Services examination, the writing skill is considered to be the basis of success.

A command over the writing skill cannot be achieved in a day. The most effective way of improving one's writing skill is ' the continuous practice'. We know very well the proverb, *"Practice makes a man perfect"*.

Therefore, start practicing the writing skill by identifying your strengths and weaknesses. The biggest challenge to the aspirants, while practicing the writing skill, is that they do not know how to start it. They think, 'I do not know how to write', 'To achieve the level of the writing skill as the UPSC Toppers have is a far-fetched thing', ' I will never be able to learn to write in a good way.', 'I can never achieve the same writing skill as the UPSC Toppers have' etc.

To clarify such apprehensions, I would like to quote William Faulkner, a writer, "Get it down, take chances.

It may be bad, but it's the only way you can do anything really good".

The best way to overcome the doubts and confusions regarding the beginning of your writing practice is that you must stop thinking whether your writing practice is bad or good. Just start writing, and you will realize that your writing skill is improving fast. You have to continue your writing practice in all the conditions, whether it is improving or not,i.e.,if your writing skill is improving, it will increase your expression level gradually; and if it is not improving, even then, your continued writing practice will improve your writing skills dramatically and qualitatively. You can improve your writing skill and take it to the level of excellence by adopting the following methods:

1. Form the habit of writing regularly, and never leave this habit. If this habit becomes a part of your routine, you can improve your performance as well as your mark sheet extraordinarily.
2. After writing the answers/essays/case studies, get them evaluated from time to time by your good and experienced friend/your guide, or at the test series, if you have joined any. If you follow this method regularly, you will realize that your writing skill is improving with each passing day. This method will provide you a positive motivation and also the advice and inputs for improving this skill.
3. The third most important thing is that you cannot learn a good writing skill by merely doing the writing practice. For this, you have to develop a general reading habit. There is a saying, "Imitation is a quality of human psychology". Hence, by reading the good text books and the famous books of the good and famous authors or some reputed magazines,the art of good writing will naturally start developing in you. Keep in mind that you need not become a poet, author, litterateur to

qualify in the Civil Services examination;you just need to learn the writing skill which matches with the level and expectations of the examiner.

4. The formula to improve your writing skill qualitatively is that you should adopt an inclusive, integrated and overall view while writing. Try to write in a balanced manner. Every coin has two sides and the truth lies somewhere in between them. Hence, avoid any kind of extreme view. Further, at the time of learning the writing skill, develop the art of writing in the 'inclusive style', i.e., include almost all the aspects related to the topic or question. If you use this style effectively,you will be able to express more ideas in less words. Remember, you can learn it through practice only.
5. In this context, the most important point is the skill of connecting things. 'Connecting the dots' is a very useful skill. For instance, the aspirants, who can connect the theoretical as well as the practical aspects of a subject through practice, get better marks than the of the other aspirants do. Besides, the art of connecting the various economic, social, scientific, cultural, philosophical aspects with one another can take your writing level towards the excellence. Remember, do not follow a specialist approach in this practice, follow a generalist approach instead.
6. The art of summarizing the points (précis) or expanding the points (expansion) is another important dimension of the writing skills. In the Civil Services examination, it may happen that you have less knowledge about a topic, but the word limit of its answer is more;or you have the full knowledge of a question, but are asked to write its answer in only 150-200 words. In such situations, you must learn the art of expanding

less information in more words or limiting more knowledge in less words.It will be very helpful to you.

Apart from improving your writing skill, if you learn the ways of improving your expression and presentation also, you will score more marks in the examination.

How to Improve your Presentation?

A good presentation of ideas is the key to fetch good marks. Have you ever thought why there remains a difference of marks between two aspirants, though they possess the same knowledge and put in the same efforts? The reason behind this difference is that both differ in their manner of presenting the content in their answer. To learn the art of presentation, you must follow the following points:

1. Write in a clear and well arranged manner. It means that your content should have a clarity as well as your answer should be neat and clean. It leaves a good impression on the examiner. For example, a lot of cutting, while writing, leaves a negative impact.
2. Try to avoid the spelling mistakes. Being a graduate, you are supposed to know the spellings correctly.
3. The aspirants are often found confused about their own hand writing. The Commission, in its guidelines, has instructed that the handwriting of the candidates should be legible. Therefore, you are expected to write neatly in a good handwriting.
4. The current pattern of the syllabus for the Civil Services examination demands a fast writing speed. To attempt the paper completly, you should practise writing the answers with full speed; and for obtaining the better marks, you should try to attempt the complete paper, which is possible only if your writing speed is fast. Therefore, practise

writing fast, but at the same time, maintain the readability.

5. Write in paragraphs, otherwise it becomes very difficult for the examiner to read and comprehend your answer. Get the sample copies of UPSC answer booklets, and practise writing your answer in paragraphs. Remember, the paragraph should not be very lengthy.You should begin a new paragraph with a new idea.
6. I suggest you to strictly follow the word limit. You must not write a lengthy answer for one question at the cost of the other questions. Besides, try to conclude your answer within the prescribe word limit, no matter if it falls short by 20-25 words. This strategy will help you in answering all the questions asked in the paper.Apart from this, you must form a general idea of the number of words you can write on one page. It will help you in following the prescribed word limit. Never count the words, written in your answers,while sitting in the examination hall. Do not worry if you write 10-20 words more or less than the prescribed word limit.
7. Write in a well organized and sequential manner. For getting a flow in your writing, you must not write haphazardly. My suggestion is that if you fall short of time in the exam hall, then form an outline in your mind,and write the same in an organized and sequential manner. While writing the Essay paper, you will get enough time to form an outline, but generally in the General Studies or the Optional Subject papers, such facility is not available. Therefore, try to write even the answers of 150-200 words in an organized manner, as it will help you in obtaining good marks. You can give the introduction and conclusion in two or three lines.

8. Now-a-days, the Question-cum-Answer-booklets in the new pattern are provided in the General Studies and Essay papers. In this booklet, a space is given after each question for writing the answers. You must try to answer the questions in the same sequence, as is given in the question paper, because the new pattern does not permit to alter the sequence of your answers,where as the old pattern did. In the old pattern, the aspirants used to write the answers of those questions first, which they knew very well.
9. Another doubt, which crops up in the mind of an aspirant, is about the type of language to be used while writing the answers. The command over a language does not mean that you need to use the literary and decorative words. It is better to focus on the flow of your language.

In short, it can be said that,"*Where there is will, there is a way*". It means, if you have the will to improve your writing skill, you can find the way to do it. A continuous hard work, dedication and will power is the only way to improve your writing skill. Your step, taken towards the direction of improving your writing skill, will fetch you very good marks in the examination.

❑❑

12

Personality Test: How to Express Yourself

Preparations for the Interview of the Civil Services Examination is very crucial, as it decides your rank in the final selection. The interview (personality test) carries 275 marks. The fact is that the marks obtained by the aspirants in the interview vary, i.e., one aspirant obtains 225 marks out of 275 marks, while the other gets only 125 marks. This huge gap between the marks obtained impacts your final merit.

With regard to the preparations for the interview, some aspirants do not find the need to prepare for the interview. They think that the knowledge they have is sufficient for appearing in the interview. Remember, the interview is in reality a personality test. Any person's personality can not be built in few days or months. The knowledge acquired since childhood, the upbringing and experience together build your overall personality. Hence, you should refine and improve your personality by doing practice and hard work. You must devote some of your time for the preparations of interview.

After appearing in the Mains exam, some aspirants waste many months in speculating and calculating the result. If you are thinking that you will prepare for the interview only after seeing the mains exam result, then it is quite possible that you may get only one week or one month time for its preparations. Undoubtedly, you cannot do the complete preparation of interview in such a short span of time, but still, you can try to remove some of your shortcomings and can refine your personality. I will once again reiterate that keep preparing for the interview even before the declaration of the mains exam result, and do not delay it.

The Objective of the Interview (Personality Test)

The Interview of the Civil Services Examination is conducted at the UPSC building situated in Delhi. Your interview will be taken by any of the various Interview Boards, constituted for this purpose. The chairman of every Interview Board is the member of the Union Public Service Commission. Generally, an Interview Board is comprised of one chairman and four other members.

The interview board is entrusted with the responsibility of testing the suitability of the aspirants for a career in the Civil Services. In my understanding, the Interview in the Civil Services examination is meant to know: how is your personality, how do you think, how do you behave and how much you desire to learn. The Interview Board wants to test your mental abilities as well as your socio-practical qualities,i.e., mental awareness, clear and logical expression, balanced view, leadership skill, integrity, awareness towards the subjects of common interest and daily events. Besides testing the aspirant's language, the choice of words and patience are also tested. In my understanding, an aspirant should have a certain level of the developed qualities, like maturity, logical attitude, communication skills, a detailed and broad base of accumulated knowledge, positivity, presence of mind, balanced view etc.

Preparations for Interview

You must not worry about your preparations for the interview before appearing in the Mains examination. After appearing in the examination, if you are optimistic about clearing it, then start the preparations for interview. Keep in mind that there is no need to hurry, as you will get sufficient time after the mains exam for the preparation of interview.

You are advised to adopt the following ways for the preparations of Interview:

- First of all go through your Detailed Application Form (DAF), which you had filled for the Mains examination. Whatever information the Interview Board has about you, your DAF is the source of that information. Therefore, make an outline of your preparations according to DAF (as far as the filling of the DAF form before the mains exam is concerned, then it has already been discussed in the chapter of this book, 'How to Perform Well in the Mains Exam')
- DAF consists of various information about you,i.e.,your name, address, home town, educational and technical qualifications, experience, interest, optional subjects and service and cadre preferences. You should start preparing the information mentioned in DAF, after appearing in the Mains exam. Prepare very well on each and every point of your bio-data. Utilize your leisure time by maintaining a diary and writing all the probable questions related to your personal information mentioned in DAF, and prepare its answers too. There may be a wide range of questions, which can be asked from your bio-data,i.e.,the questions related to the meaning of your name, your qualities,the problems of your home district and home state, your educational qualifications and other relevant issues related to your optional subjects.
- The aspirants remain too much tense about the questions related with their own interests, which they have mentioned in their DAF. Firstly,you should write only those hobbies and interests in the application form, which you are connected with for quite some time,like playing any sports, reading books, listening music, watching movies,

doing meditation, writing poetry etc. Prepare the questions very well, related to your one or two hobbies. Do some reading on it. During your interview preparations, you should devote half an hour to your hobbies daily. Only then, you will connect deeply with that hobby and will feel comfortable during the interview.

- Another major aspect of interview preparations is Current Affairs and the issues related to it. The Interview Board may want to know your views and thinking, but for this purpose a topic or a subject is needed on which both the parties can have a discussion. The Current Affairs becomes quite important from this point of view.The events one month before the interview and the issues related to those events become extremely important in this regard. Therefore, for preparing the Interview, I would suggest you to maintain a diary and make a brief notes about the important national and international issues of that period in it.
- During the interview preparations, it is very necessary to be aware of your surroundings. For this, you can take the help of radio, TV, newspapers, magazines and internet. Integrate all the mediums and use them.
- The Interview Board can ask about your views on some controversial issues,e.g., 'Whether the policy of alcohol ban is right or wrong', 'Whether the homosexuality is immoral', 'Whether the communalism has increased in India ' etc. Note the pros and cons of such issues, and then come to a conclusion. Whatever the conclusion is, in my understanding, it should be progressive and positive. It should not be extreme.
- Try to give some mock interviews before appearing in the final interview, as by doing so

you will come to know about your shortcomings which you yourself had no idea about. Although some aspirants who did not give a single mock interview, had scored good marks in the interview, but you should try to face other interviews also, before appearing in the interview of the Civil Services examination.

- For giving the mock interviews, it is suggested to form a group of three or four friends, and those two or three friends should take the interview of the fourth friend. In this manner, the preparations of your interview will not be limited to the closed doors. You should prepare regularly for the interview through the group discussions and mock interviews.
- You must also keep in mind that if the interviewer in the mock interview points out at any big shortcoming of you, then you must not over think or lose your confidence, you should try to improve it instead. It may be the case that your particular shortcoming appears big to the person who is interviewing in the mock interview, but the UPSC interview board may not give much importance to that particular shortcoming.

Preparations Just before the Interview

Keep the following things in mind just before the interview:

- Make ready your formal dress. For the male aspirants, wearing a light colored shirt, black or dark colored trousers, tie and the formal black shoes is a better option. Similarly for the female aspirants, wearing a plain Saree or Salwar-suit is better. The aspirants should dress-up in a simple and formal dress, irrespective of their gender.
- Remain calm just before the interview day. Do not take stress of your studies. If someone gives a suggestion at the last moment, do not get affected

by it. Prior to the interview, you will come across such persons who will ask you whether you have prepared a certain topic or not. If you have not prepared that particular topic, then do not take its stress. It is not necessary that the same question will be asked in the interview. Try to avoid the pessimistic persons during this period.

- Sleep well and wake up with a fresh mind. Take care of your health, and eat light and easily digestive food. Do not skip your breakfast.
- Arrange all the documents which the Commission has asked you to bring for the interview, and keep it safely. Otherwise, at the last moment or in the UPSC building, you will start panicking and losing confidence.

How to Face the Interview Board?

The Interview is conducted in two shifts: morning and afternoon shifts. Firstly, all your original documents (which have been demanded) are verified at the UPSC headquartersin Delhi. To avoid the last minute confusion, arrange your documents in a well organized manner at home itself. You will be asked to sit on your table in a hall, where other aspirants are also sitting. Do not go into any detailed discussion with them. Of course, you can introduce yourself or exchange smiles in order to feel comfortable. Never underestimate yourself by thinking that a certain aspirant is more qualified than you, or you have less knowledge than the other one has.

The following are some important tips to face the Interview Board:

- Enter the interview room, and sit comfortably after taking permission of the board. Neither lean too much nor sit too straight.
- While facing the interview, your mind should be open; be at ease; and be that person what actually you are.

- Keep in mind that you should never try to bluff or mislead the members of the Interview Board, as they are very experienced people. By providing them any wrong information, you can get stuck in the forthcoming questions. They have a very long experience in doing this job. Never pretend, remain easy.
- Remember that you should maintain a balanced approach while answering the questions.
- Another important thing is that listen to the question of that member of the Interview Board very carefully and patiently, who is putting the question to you. You may request to repeat the question, if you fail to understand it, but never try to start answering before listening to the question completely.
- The value of humility is precious and proves to be very useful during the interview; but remember that an excess of it will appear like a meekness.
- If you feel that you do not have any idea or clue about a particular question, humbly accept it;but if you do have some idea on that issue, answer the question by taking a prior permission of the board. I mean to say, you should not give up in this manner.
- During the interview, speak in a clear voice. You should be neither too loud nor too low. You must not get excited or feel nervous while answering the questions. There are many aspirants who, during the interview, feel that their interview is not going well, but when the result comes, they obtain very good marks. Therefore, try to keep a light smile on your face.

❑❑

13

Never Never Never Give Up

Raja Ganpati Ramasamy: He reached Chennai to prepare for the Civil Services Examination, after completing his studies in the Medical College. In the first attempt, he failed to focus on his preparations. Many doubts and confusions used to haunt him. Whenever he used to be tense, his father's face would come in front of his eyes. Raja's father had come to see off his son, believing that his son would become an I.A.S in his very first attempt. However, Raja gave the first attempt without full preparations. The result of the Preliminary examination was not favorable. Gradually, his friends started settling down in their lives. Some sort of frustration started creeping in, but he was still studying. Even the relatives started questioning his father that why his son was not working. However, his father still believed that his son would become an I.A.S in his second attempt.

The 'C-SAT' paper was introduced in the syllabus during Raja's second attempt. He was already weak in the mathematics, so he could not succeed even in his second attempt,and failed to qualify in the prelims exam. Now the situation became worst. He could not gather the courage of borrowing money from his family for continuing his study, as he felt guilty. He started writing in a competitive magazine, and in return he started earning some money. His relatives used to put pressure on his family to get him married, but Raja still did not have a job. One day, Raja's mother cried a lot in front of him and asked him to leave the Civil Services preparations, and get a permanent job;

but Raja had always dreamt of becoming an I.A.S, thus he started a teaching job and started earning a respectable money.

Then he gave the third attempt but he failed in this attempt too. Raja's fate was not in his favor, and the pressure was increasing from all sides. He wept without tears and learnt to face the adversities and inequalities of life. While giving the fourth attempt, Raja had full faith that this time he would succeed in the prelims exam, but unfortunately, he could not clear the prelims exam even in this fourth attempt. Raja's strong- willed father cried for the first time in front of him;but at the same time, Raja passed P.C.S exam of State Public Service Commission with 15th rank.With the help of this platform, he decided that he would give his fifth attempt of the Civil Services examination. Raja's elder brother motivated him. This time he succeeded in the prelims, the mains exam as well as in the interview. Raja Ganpati Ramasamy, who got success in the Civil Services Examination, 2014, in his fifth attempt, was allotted an I.A.S Uttar Pradesh cadre. Raja considers his story as 'the story of success after many failures'. He gives a message to all the aspirants:

'Never, never, never give up'!

Rajender Paensiya: Rajendra hailed from Shriganganagar district, a small town of Rajasthan. He had never been a topper in his class; he obtained around 52 percent marks in the High School and 60 percent marks in the Intermediate. Rajendra was a student of Hindi medium, and he grew up in an environment where most of the people dreamt of getting the job of a Patwari or a Teacher. Some people suggested him to do the B.Ed., as it would be beneficial for him. Therefore, he completed the B.Ed. degree and became a Third Grade Teacher.

After he became a teacher, someone suggested him to try for the Rajasthan Administrative Services (R.A.S). Though he did not believe that he could ever be an R.A.S officer, but still he decided to appear in its exam. For the first time in his life, he came to a big city like Jaipur. In his first attempt, he got a rank, which was beyond the 600th rank. Not knowing how to lose hope,he made efforts to improve his rank; and in his second and third attempt, he secured the 115th rank and 8th rank respectively.

Now he started dreaming to become an I.A.S. He moved to Delhi. He started appearing in UPSC examinations. In his first attempt, he reached up to the stage of interview, but could not be selected in the final merit; in his second attempt he again reached up to the interview;and in his third attempt, he failed to clear even the prelims exam. In his fourth attempt, he cleared the prelims exam but failed to clear the mains exam;but he did not lose the hope of becoming an I.A.S. Finally, he got selected in the final merit of the Civil Services Examination, 2014. He secured the 345th rank, and he was allotted the I.A.S Uttar Pradesh cadre. He had a simple formula, that was 'persistence'.

Ghanshyam Meena: He was an engineering graduate and hailed from Jaipur. He always dreamt of becoming a Civil Servant. He tried for both the Rajasthan Administrative Services and the Indian Administrative Services examinations. Fortunately, he got selected in the Department of Sales Tax in the Rajasthan Administrative Services, but in his first attempt, he failed to clear even the prelims exam, conducted by the Union Public Service Commission. In his second attempt, He reached up to the stage of the Mains exam. When the result was declared, he came to know that he had failed to qualify the Compulsory Hindi paper. Along with his job, he used to do his UPSC preparations daily in the evening as well as in the weekends. In his third attempt, he got a call for the interview. In his fourth attempt, he succeeded in the prelims as well as in the mains exam. He gave his interview in the Hindi medium, and finally got selected. He was allotted an I.A.S Bihar Cadre of 2015 batch. Ghanshyam believes that the mantra of his success is the positive thinking and the will to continue efforts in spite of failures.

Beno Zephine: The completely blind Beno Zaifin was a Probationary Officer in the State Bank of India. She was very active since her childhood. Participating in various debate competitions was her hobby. Beno started preparing for the Civil Services Examination, but there was a great dearth of study materials in the Braille script. Beno never let her disability obstruct the way of her preparations; and finally, she got selected in the Civil Services Examination. Beno is very social and humble. Today, she has become the first blind officer of the Indian Foreign Service (IFS); and presently, she is undergoing the training. Beno gave the credit of her success to her parents, especially to her friends, who used to read books for her for long durations.

Pooja Kumari Parth: She grew up in a common family which had five siblings,i.e., two elder and two younger. Her father is a Librarian. She and her father both dreamt together that she would become an I.A.S one day. Her father gave her full guidance, but never pressurized her. He used to bring good books and magazines, and she used to study,comprehend and absorb them with full dedication.

She passed B.A. in history, sociology and philosophy. Since she could not fill the form of the Civil Services examination till she attained 21 years of age, she did her post-graduation in Sociology. Besides appearing in the various competitive examinations, she continued her preparations for the Civil Services examination too. She passed the Patwari exam and the prelims exam of the State Services (R.A.S). She selected Sociology as her optional subject and decided to write in Hindi medium. Pooja has set a unique record by obtaining 163rd rank in the Civil Services Examination, 2014. She had never joined any coaching and had never given any mock interview. She had achieved this success by dint of her hard work, courage and dedication.

Sachin Kumar Vaish: Sachin Kumar Vaish hailed from Pratapgarh district of Uttar Pradesh. He achieved 94th rank in the Civil Services Examination, 2014. His story of success gives a message that if a struggle is done with simplicity, it can take you towards an extraordinary success. Despite of all the economic and social problems, his father funded for his studies. He failed to get admission in an I.I.T. Therefore, he took admission in a U.P.T.U college, and continued his studies with the support of his family and relatives.

The Destiny tested him several times, and he failed in different examinations many times,i.e., he failed in SCRA Examination and also in GATE. In spite of failures, he never gave up. He came to Delhi and started his preparations for the Civil Services. He selected 'Public Administration' as his optional subject. He gave the examination in the English medium and achieved a good rank in his very first attempt by dint of his regular studies and revision.

My own story is not different from the above stories of success. I hail from Meerut (Uttar Pradesh). I have studied in the school and colleges in the Hindi medium.Getting the 13th rank in the Civil Services Examination, 2014, like a dream come true to me. None of my family members or relatives have been in the Civil Services, nor they ever dare to see such a big dream. I dreamt big, but the resources were not available to me. I did B.A. in history, political science and English and M.A. in Hindi from Meerut. Later on, I did M.Phil from the University of Delhi.

I have worked as a Translator in the Lok Sabha Secretariat also. In my first attempt in 2012, I could not pass even the prelims exams of I.A.S and UPPCS. Not being used to such failures, I became highly disappointed. However, due to the motivation of my friends and family, I secured 13th Rank in the Civil Services Examination, 2014; and also succeeded in obtaining 1053 marks out of 1500 marks in the mains exam of UPPCS, 2014.

The above examples give an important message to the aspirants that it is but natural for them to reach the stage of prelims exam, mains exam or interview in several attempts, but they should not stop their efforts and should keep trying to achieve success in the Civil Services examination. We have learnt the following things from these stories:

In our life,the basic mantra of success is 'Persistence'. Presently, the persistence quotient of the aspirants is judged in the various examinations. It is very easy to start a task, but to do that task regularly is very tough. We often meet such aspirants, who make very good plans, but when they are supposed to implement their multi-level plans,most of them get lazy and just idle away their time. Therefore, never forget the mantra of 'persistence', and keep progressing towards the path of success.

Another thing is that you should not have excessive expectations, as the nature of this highly competitive exam is such that no one can guarantee a definite success in all the three stages of the examination.

I have read somewhere that there is a wing in the army of a country, where it is mandatory for the aspirants to have tasted failure at least once in their life in order to join that wing. This wing believes that the person, who does not know how to overcome the disappointment of the failures, will never be able to face the adverse situations boldly. I have learnt more from my single failure (failure in the prelims exam in my first attempt) than from the successes achieved in my whole life. Yugal ji, the spiritual poet in Hindi, has written the following inspiring lines in his poem:

"When the bad days of your life are going on,
the river of hope dries,
When man's simple and calm nature becomes
the mirage of the desert.
When my physical body takes its last breath,
Has anyone been able to extinguish
the light of my knowledge?
In the doom's day of the world,
my inner light still glows,
In the curses the golden flowers of boons blooms".

We know that the still water gets stale, in the same manner the life, which is devoid of activities, becomes burdensome. The proverb, 'Nothing succeeds like success' says that the failures and adversities in one's life should not matter.You should neither get tired nor stop after the failures. The wheel of time keeps revolving regardless of your success and failures. Therefore, you must plan an optional career too in your life, apart from the Civil Services. An optional career in the government or private sector will help you in remaining stress-free and pressure-free during your preparations. I feel that you should be prepared for the adverse result, even after giving your best performance in the examination, as it makes you more strong. The following English proverb is very relevant in the present context:

"Try for the best, Prepare for the worst".

You should not stop your preparations when when you are near to the success. The preparations for the Civil Services examination demands a certain level of maturity. You should not lose hope when you are about to attain that maturity level. The following quotation by Thomas Alva Edison is very relevant here:

"Many of life's failure are people, who did not realize how close they were to success when they gave up".

The above stories convey one more mantra of success : the 'indomitable spirit' of the successful aspirants It is the 'indomitable spirit' which maintained the morale and motivation level of these aspirants. The positivity and motivation will be required not only for the preparation of the Civil Services Examination, but also for the other tests of your life. Therefore, build a positive atmosphere and try to avoid negativity, depression and frustration. We all remember the proverb, 'All is well that ends well',but you must not forget the following lines also:

"Adverse situations come in everyone's life,
Some persons get shattered,
Some persons do improvise:

There is one special quality in the personality of the successful aspirants,i.e., they never let their dreams die despite of the lack of resources, their physical disability or any other shortcoming. Besides, they manage their failures so well that they finally attain success. They do not get distracted during the failures, and handle the success very well when they achieve it. They continue their further journey as per the motto, *"Success is a journey, not a destination"*.

❑❑

14 Beyond the Stars are Even More Worlds: Civil Services Exam Vs. Other Career Options

I have observed that the aspirants, who come from the middle class, lower middle class or from economically weak background, remain very tense and confused. They have many apprehensions about their success, i.e., if they are not selected in the Civil Services, what will happen to them, what they will do then, how they will face their families,how they will lead their lives etc. Some of them take so much tension that they become the victims of anxiety and possessiveness.They feel that if they do not become an I.A.S, their lives will be useless, and after that there will be no other aim of their lives.

These aspirants think so, because they have not planned for any other suitable career option, apart from the Civil Services.. I agree with the fact that it is necessary for an aspirant to possess the dedication, perseverance, devotion and concentration; but one should possess a another career option also to avoid this type of tension, depression, speculation and confusion. If you possess another career option, or you know that you have the eligibility and employability to earn a respectable living and lead a good life even in the adverse conditions, when you are actually not selected in the Civil Services; then definitely you will feel calm and relaxed.

I want to make it clear in this regard that, having another career option is not compulsory for doing the preparations of the Civil Services examination, and there are numerous examples of the aspirants who have done the preparations of this examination considering it as their only career option, and they have been successful too; but it is a wise decision to have another career option and employability, keeping in mind the uncertainty and cut-throat competition for getting selected in the Civil Services.Therefore, it is better to remain free from such a useless tension and pressure, and do the preparations in a natural manner.

You must have heard the saying,"Try for the best, prepare for the worst".

Therefore, to keep a career option in mind is a better way to handle such a situation. Let us discuss some of the career options to lead a good life, in case you do not get selected in the Civil Services. This strategy is also known as a 'backup plan'. Remember the famous proverb,"Don't put all eggs in one basket". So you should not limit your efforts to just one career optionyou should look for another career option instead, which suits your interests, expectations and abilities. Some of the suggested career options for such aspirants are given below:

(I) Other competitive exams of UPSC: According to their eligibility and aptitude, the aspirants of Civil Services can appear in the following examinations also, which are conducted every year by the Union Public Service Commission:

(i) Indian Forest Service
(ii) Indian Engineering Service
(iii) Indian Statistical Service
(iv) Indian Economic Service
(v) Central Medical Service
(vi) Central Police Force, Assistant Commandant

All the above mentioned examinations are Group 'A' services of Government of India, which are extremely prestigious and challenging career options.

(II) Examinations of State Public Service Commission(s): The public service commission of various states of India conduct the examinations for the various Gazetted/Non-Gazetted posts of Group 'A' and Group 'B' also, apart from conducting their own State Civil Service Examinations. Besides, the Public Service Commission of various states issue the advertisements for the other posts too from time to time. I am sure that you can prepare for your home state Civil Services Examination (P.C.S) along with the Civil Services preparations. I too had done the preparations for the Uttar Pradesh P.C.S., along with the preparations of the Civil Services. Generally, the syllabus of the State Civil Services examination contains one paper of the Official Language of that state.

(III) Other different competitive examinations: In addition to the above mentioned Public Service Commission, the various board/commission of the Central and State Governments also conduct various examinations:-

(i) Parliament of India (Joint Recruitment Cell)
(ii) CGL Examination of SSC
(iii) Delhi Subordinate Services Selection Board
(iv) Railway Recruitment Board
(v) State Bank of India and Institute of Banking Personnel Selection. (IBPS)

These secompetitive examinations provide a respectable career option. Interestingly, these examinations too offer the subjects, like general knowledge, English, reasoning and mathematics, which are more or less similar to that of UPSC C-SAT.

(IV) Other career options: The other attractive career options for the aspirants, who are preparing their backup plan, are as following:

(i) UGC-NET-JRF (teaching and research work): It is a very respectable career. I had also cleared NET-JRF in Hindi Literature in my first attempt and got its fellowship, and did the M.Phil also from the University of Delhi.

(ii) Media and Mass Communication
(iii) Advertisement and Public Relation
(iv) Radio and T.V.
(v) Interpretation and Translation
(vi) You can be an entrepreneur and start your own business.In this way, you will give employment to others, and can play a role in the nation building.
(vii) Another emerging career option is Social Work. By joining a good NGO or doing part-time job in this sector, you will earn some money as well as you can contribute in the development of the society. In order to gain a social experience, many aspirants do the social-work during the period they get after giving the mains exam and before appearing in the interview.

(V) **Further studies through the distance learning mode:** Some of the aspirants while doing the Civil Services Examination preparations or after completing their preparations, continue their further studies through the distance education mode. It has three benefits: firstly, you will be able to improve your profile in the years, which are otherwise considered as gap years; secondly, you can get a help in your Optional Subject or G.S. and thirdly, after attaining the degree/diploma, the chances of your employability and the level of your confidence will increase.

The Indira Gandhi National Open University offers the best course options in the distance education mode.All the more,the study material of IGNOU courses is is excellent. I It can help you to a great extent in the preparations of your optional subject.

Besides IGNOU, you can do further studies through the distance learning mode from the State Open Universities also.

In addition to the above courses, you can do some recognized computer courses, like P.G. Diploma in Computer Applications (PGDCA) and DOEACC.

Keep in mind,you must not get confused after getting involved in these optional career options. You should not get distracted from your main and primary focus area. I have informed you about these alternate career/ study options, so that you can understand that, 'beyond the stars are even more worlds'.Your life should never halt or stop, even if you fail in a particular examination on a particular day. Moving ahead continuously following the mantra of 'Keep going- Keep going' is the essence of life. In this context, the following poem of Gopal Das 'Niraj' is very relevant for the youths:

" O thee who stealthily shed tears!
Who waste these pearls of their eye!
If some dreams cease to be Life doesn't end, it doesn't die

What's a dream? Just a dew-drop,
On your eye, amidst a siesta deep,
And its dissipation is as if,
Youth is woken-up mid-sleep,
O thee who make their lives moist
Who bathe, but don't immerse, why!
If some water flows out and away Monsoon
doesn't end, it doesn't die.

So what if the beads scattered,
The problem is resolved per se,
If your tears are auctioned off,
Then your penance is complete.
O thee who spend their days glum!
who sew their torn shirts and cry,
If some lamps get extinguished,
the porch stays, it doesn't die.

Nothing gets lost here,
The book changes its cover,
Like the night peels moonlight,
In the morn to be sun-ray lover.
O thee who change clothes and come,
who go, but in new pomp and style,
If lost is the moon you thought a toy,
childhood doesn't end, it doesn't die.

Many, many pots n pails have broken,
Not a crease on the well's face of muscle.
Many, many boats have sunk,
The shore has the same hustle-bustle.
O thee who extend the darkness,
Who reduce the life of light,
Fall may try, and then try,
The orchard lives, it doesn't die.

The gardener pillaged the garden,
Flower's fragrance couldn't be stolen.
Even storms tried playing with it,
But window of dust would remain open.
O thee who embrace hatred, who throw dirt on every guy,
Even if some faces are upset the mirror stays, it doesn't die.

❑❑

15

The Untold Stories of Success

"Winners don't do the different things,
They do the things differently".

Such persons exist amongst us, who do not get affected by the favorable or unfavorable circumstances, and do not care about the various kinds of problems (educational, social or economic). They not only dream big, but also make their dreams come true by the dint of their dedication and devotion. Such untold stories are not known to you, as they have never been told. These persons, in spite of facing numerous struggles, have made new records. Every story is unique in itself. These young talents, who come from a different region and social-cultural background, have shared not only the inspiring stories of their struggle but also the strategies to overcome such struggles. A poet has reflected the struggle story of these aspirants in the following expressions:

"If you want to judge their talents,
Then you must make the sky a bit higher".

The following poem, written by me, is dedicated to the optimism of these young talents:

Perhaps light is still far...

With each passing Diwali,
Let candles be lighted, let Rangoli shine.
With fireworks and chandeliers,
Let each lane and home shine.

But some eyes are barren,
And some dreams are unfulfilled.

Some cute faces too,
Look at their corridors.

Some homes seem deserted,
Some faces lack radiance.
Some lazy eyes search,
Perhaps light is still far.

Let those tired eyes,
Be filled with some happiness.
Let some sweetness reach to them,
Let some of their pains be lessened.

Some happiness and some smiles,
Unfurling in each barren house.
Smiles and laughters,
Will merge with one's voice...

Only then this darkness will vanish,
Only then the devoid faces will glow.
Only then every eye will be lightened,
Only then the golden dreams will bloom.

Ajitesh Meena
(Rajasthan)
IRS 2015

Ajitesh Meena: If I lookback the 24 years of my life, prior to the selection, through the bioscope, then the journey of this long struggle in such a short period fills my eyes with tears. I was born in a farmer's family at Ghanoli, a small village in Sawai Madhopur. Though my father was a graduate, but his bad habit of drinking has converted him into a completely irresponsible person. When I became mature enough to understand all this, I realized that all my lands were sold off by him, and only 4 Bighas of land are left with us.We were in huge debts. In the name of the property, we inherited a small collection of a few novels, biographies, poetry collections and history books.

Every year during the summer vacations, I used to go near the river to graze our buffaloes. I used to carry four-six books with me, which I could finish till the evening. Once, I get so much immersed in studying that my buffaloes moved several miles ahead. I also used to work in the field, according to my capacity. After completing my studies till Class VIII in my village's government school, I studied in a government school till class XII from, which was in Surval town, five k.ms ahead of my village. I used to go to the school with my twin brother Amitesh by the same bicycle, and while returning from school, I used to carry a bundle of grass with me.

Despite of facing several hardships, my mother and grandmother somehow managed to arrange money for all my five siblings' education. Whenever I needed money I borrowed it from my grandmother. If she did not have that much of money with her, she used to say that, "Just eat your food son, I will arrange the money"; and she used to arrange the money in a magical way. Later I taught the students in my elder brother's tuition classes and earned some money. The happiness once again returned in my family, when I was in B.A. Part-I and I was about 19 years old, I was selected for the post of Patwari. During the nine months training I received a stipend of 1200 rupees. In two years I earned 6,100 rupees in the form of salary.This amount appeared to me like one million. The objective of my life began to take a shape, when I received my first appointment in Makrana, Nagour, where I got an opportunity to observe the administration closely. I learnt the administrative nuances by working under an honest S.D.M Shri S.M. Shah and a diligent Tahsildar Shri Suresh Chawla. The problems of the villagers and their intense complaints against the system infused a sense of sensitivity in me. As a result, during my two years service I made the people aware about the services provided by not only the revenue department but also by the other departments. At the end of the year 2012, I started preparing for R.A.S and I.A.S examinations. A good governance, serving the people, Gandhiji's philosophy and my own humble background acted as an inspiration to me.

During my studies, I faced many mental and economic problems. I always used to travel in the general coaches of the trains. In July 2015, I was selected on the posts of S.D.M in R.A.S as well as in I.R.S (Income tax) in Civil Services and I took admission in my life's first college, i.e., National Academy of Direct Taxes.

In fact, I was fortunate enough that I was blessed with my elder brother's strong discipline, my younger brother's economic support and my mother's immense love, which were much better than the wealth in a rich family. My mother always worked extremely hard, but never complained. My family and friends are still inspiring me to become a good civil servant in its true sense. Now 'May all live happily' is the main motto of my life. I pray to God seeking only the good sense from him,so that I can repay the society's debts with full interest.

Ansar Shaikh
(Maharashtra)
IAS 2016

Ansar Shaikh: I was born and brought up in a very poor and underprivileged family in a slum area of Shelgaon Village in Maharashtra's jalna. My father used to drive an auto rickshaw & my mother was a housemaker. There were literally all kinds of odds that i had to face. However i was good at studies, hence unlike my 3 siblings, i was able to persue my education. From class 1 to 10th i studied in a government school in my village. I passed 10th with 76.20 per cent marks. Then i moved to Badrinarayan Barwale College, Jalna for pursuing my 11-12th in Humanities. By this time I had made my mind to go to pune & prepare for UPSC. I scored 91.50 per cent & moved to ferguson college pune. While in second year of my BA Political science, i joined a coaching class of UPSC. I graduated in june 2015 with 73 per cent marks. In August same year, i appeared for UPSC CSE PRE which I qualified.

Hardwork was not new to me. However my poor economic background was one of the major obstacles in my journey. There was a time when i had nothing to eat for whole day, there was also a time when I didn't have money to purchase books. Language was another problem for me. I was preparing in Marathi medium however i had to read more than 60 per cent syllabus in English & translate it in marathi! This was difficult as i did my all education till 12th in Marathi medium. But there is always a solution.

I decided to be an officer while i was in 10th standard. My class teacher who cleared MPSC in the same year was one of the motivating factor along with my personal experiences. However it was my another teacher from my college who gave me basic information about UPSC, till then i was unaware of UPSC and all.

I cleared this exam in my very first attempt hence there was no such failure as far as UPSC CSE is concerned. But yes, there were failures. I faced them with a smiling face. I was self motivated hence it was easy for me to console my self and get back to the business. After all failure is a blessing in disguise! It gives you an opportunity to introspect yourself and overcome your weaknesses.

I would recommend following points to be kept in mind while preparing for CSE-

1. decide what do you exactly want to do.
2. Decide as early as possible
3. start as early as possible
4. analyse the exam pattern, syllabus etc
5. stick to basics, dont run behind n number of noted and books
6. have focus and consistency in your studies.
7. plan your journey according to your abilities, customise your preparation
8. believe in yourself, it's doable.
9. "be happy "

I want to work as much as i can for the poor people of our country. Women empowerment, rural development are other areas of my interest.

My message to the youth is-

"If an underprivileged person like me, who has faced all odds of life can do it, then you can do it too. Success in UPSC CSE is not a monopoly of anybody."

Ashish Kumar: When Nishantji asked me to write my own experiences, then I started thinking what should I write and how should I write it. It was very difficult for me to decide what I should write for this. At last, I decided to write my sweet and sour experiences and good and bad situations in life. I wish to express it in the words of a poet,"it consists of flowers as well as thorns; roses as well as mud".

Ashish Kumar
(Bihar)
IRS 2015

I still remember the day when the result of Class X's was published. I got 85 percent marks from Bihar Board, and had perhaps topped not only in my town but also in the whole region. Perhaps it is the highest marks obtained by any aspirant there, especially in my government school.

I went to study in Patna, where I started attending the mathematics classes conducted by Shri Anand Kumar. There were many problems in my life, like the economic bankruptcy of my father, two elder sisters and money for my studies. In other words, life was not a bed of roses for me. I continued my studies by studying in a nearby government school and by depositing the tuition fee with a little delay. Besides, I used to study for many hours in the nearby Book Store, but these habits made my struggle joyous.

Going to Patna and studying there was a very big challenge in itself. When I lost all hopes, at that time I came to know about a railway examination in which 40 students were selected from each zone; and after giving them Railway's Vocational Training, the railway appointed them as T.C or Clerk.

Living at the Guwahati Railway Station and doing the duty of a T.C, besides doing my studies was a very difficult task.

While doing graduation, I felt that I would not be able to continue my job as a T.C., as I was not getting a time to study. Despite of doing my duties with full honesty, the departmental inspectors always kept an eye on me, all these pressures once again lit the fire within me. At that time, I used to teach the mathematics and science to the students free of cost. One day, I met one of my friends in a lane. He was studying in the IIT. He told me that he was preparing for CAT and that I too can appear in the examination. On the very same day, I saw the advertisement of CAT programme by some institute. Fortunately, the institute was situated very near to my office.

There begins the second phase of my life. At the institute, I became familiar with the logical reasoning and mathematics. To study for several hours and do the night duty intentionally became a part of my life. My friendship with the owner of Wheeler Book Stall ended the scarcity of books and magazines for me.On the other hand, the second innings of my friendship with the books gave a new dimension to my life. When I matched my answers with the answer booklet after appearing in CAT, 2008, I thought that I would not be selected. I appeared in the SSC mains exam at the same time. However, I got calls from four IIMs. Not only this, I also got selected in SSC. My life once again came back on the right track. Perhaps, my faith in God has provided me those moments back, which I had lost already.

My interview in IIM was satisfactory, but I could not get selected due to my weak communication skills. In the year 2010, after clearing SSC examination, I joined on the post of Income Tax Inspector. I passed the examinations, like SBI, OBC, and CDS as well. I became SSC Topper in the year 2008. Now by divine intervention, I found my way to move ahead naturally in life.

At the places of my job, I met some of my friends, especially the most affectionate one, Upendranath Verma, who was doing the preparations of the Civil Services Examination for the past several years. I felt that I can do it too. In my first attempt I cleared the prelims exam. I came to live in Mukherjee Nagar, Delhi, in the year 2011. I qualified the Civil Services Exam and at present I am serving as IRS officer of 2015 Batch.

Balaji DK
(Karnataka)
IAS 2015

Balaji DK: Clearing IAS was my childhood dream. It all started when I was in 5th standard, from a fight with my dad. Dad had gotten angry on me and beaten me. I was sobbing. A GK question was asked on TV. I answered it correctly, leaving my dad very happy. He hugged me. Anger was replaced by pride and happiness. It made me realize that GK could help me win anyone. Then, I developed keen interest in GK so much so that I wanted to clear the toughest GK exam in the country (that was how I was thinking)!! Then, I was told that IAS was such an exam.

I was attending private tuition from Mr. Sachidananda Rao sir, as I fondly remember him, always used to say that one should live in such a way that atleast 4 persons should remember him/her for 4 days after death. These words strengthened my resolve to become IAS. Simultaneously, another teacher Shri Jagadishiah KS used to narrate the stories of successful IAS, IPS aspirants. It was an icing on the cake.

Then, came a breakthrough when I had just given 10th std. exam. Mr. Jagadish KJ from my hometown (Koratagere, Tumkur District, Karnataka) cleared IAS exam with AIR 58. It was a clear pointer to me that I should become the next Jagadish of my hometown. IAS dream started formally.

Then my 10th results came. I had got 93.76% with 100% marks in Mathematics. Everyone suggested that I should opt Science for my pre-University. But, my heart said that I should choose humanities to pursue my IAS dream.

As all of you are aware, Science stream offers better job opportunities. Coming from a middle class family (my father hails from a very poor family. My paternal grandfather had deserted the family. My grandmother raised my dad by working as daily wage labourer. My dad worked at multiple places and could somehow find a job in a Gramin Bank. My mother also comes from an equally humble family), finding a very good job for myself was very important for me. Yet, I wanted to pursue my IAS dream. Surprisingly, my parents stood by me and allowed me to pursue my dream. Everyone called my parents mad. Yet, they stood by me.

In the very first week of mine joining 11th std., CSR magazine hung at a book store caught my attention. The cover page of that CSR issue featured the photos of Mr. S. Nagarajan (AIR 1, CSE 2005) and Ms. Suja K (AIR 4, 2005). These pictures compelled me to pick that magazine. Alas!!! I didn't understand anything in that magazine. I then realized how bad my English was. I decided that I should first learn English to clear IAS exam. I devised my own strategy. At that time, I was traveling to college (which was in Tumkur, 26 km away) by bus daily. I decided to travel only by video-coach-buses. I started translating the dialogues of Kannada and Telugu movies into english. Whenever I encountered any difficulty, I used to write it down and get the same clarified next day with English lecturers. I always used to try forming English sentences in mind. I lived in English for 3 months. It really helped me gain a reasonable command over English language.

While in 12th std. two thoughts haunted me repeatedly.

a. What if I don't clear IAS? Will I be able to settle in life?

b. I could read these humanities subjects on my own. Should have I to pursue it as a regular course? Or should have I to pursue any other professional course?

Then, my college Principal Mr. N.P. Ravindranath cleared all confusion, infused confidence in me. He suggested me to pursue Bachelor of Business Management (BBM) and then do MBA.

After my MBA, I got to know of a community organization that offered free boarding, lodging and coaching for IAS aspirants. When I approached them, I was humiliated. It again strengthened my resolve.

For UPSC aspirants, I would share some of the important strategies in brief–

The mantra for prelims is to *read-revise-recall*. Whenever I read for prelims, I tried thinking about the questions that could emerge from that section.

The mantra for mains is Writing Practice. I suggest aspirants to write a test every alternate day. It is advisable to write tests for less-than-maximum-time. That is, one has to write a 250 marks paper in 2 hrs 30 mins.

The second important thing is try to support your arguments with some statistic, research findings. You find them in 'The Hindu'. Only thing is that you should be smart enough to identify them.

With regard to essay, one should remember that it has to be analytical. Try to examine the causes, effects, problems and solutions pertaining to the essay topic. Don't just give examples from various fields to support the essay topic. I committed this mistake in my first attempt and ended up with a paltry 70 marks. I wish you don't fall victim to this mistake of mine.

Last suggestion from my side—Don't run behind many books for the same topic. Remember that reading one book twice is better than reading two books, each once.

Devi Lal: A majority of India's youths dream of joining the Civil Services. I too have seen the same dream. I received my primary school education in a small village of Barmer, a backward district, which is situated in the western desert of Rajasthan. My father was a teacher.For providing his children a better education, he moved to a city, leaving the village behind.As a result, my further schooling was done in the city. I did my intermediate from a government school, and did my B.Sc. from Barmer College. Although I have dreamt of becoming a Civil Servant since my childhood, but I started preparing for the Civil Services only after completing my graduation. In the beginning, I faced many problems, like what to study and what not to study,how to improve my writing skill etc. Besides, learning English for the Hindi medium aspirants was a challenge, but I accepted this challenge and learnt English, because the good study materials were available in English only.

Devi Lal
(Rajasthan)
IAS 2016

I gave my first attempt in the year 2012, and cleared the prelims exam; but I failed in the mains exam. I learnt from my mistakes and gave my second attempt in 2013. This time I cleared both the prelims and mains exam but could not get selected in the final merit. In 2014, I was selected in the final merit, but the dream of becoming an I.A.S was not fulfilled. In 2015, I gave my fourth attempt, and finally my dream of becoming an I.A.S came true.

My early failures disappointed me; but deep in my heart, I always had a hope that I would definitely succeed, if not this time then certainly the next time; and I would not accept the defeat before achieving my target. I used to thinkif other aspirants could get success why I could not However, I have never thought of doing any other job, but keeping in mind the uncertainties of the Civil Services, it is wise to think about another career option too.

According to the demands of the time UPSC is continuously bringing changes in its examination pattern. In such a situation, the new aspirants should also make modifications in their strategy as per the demands of the commission. The most important thing in the UPSC preparations is to avoid the memorizing things, and instead, one should try to comprehend things and keep oneself abreast of the current affairs.

As of now, one stage of my life has been completed. I must prepare myself for future. As I say that it is important to pass this examination, but the more important thing is get an opportunity to serve the country and the society and face the challenges while doing this service. I will always try to contribute something to the country and society by doing my duty with dedication, honesty and sensitivity. I request all the readers that they should initiate the change which they want to see in the society. If you are positive while possessing a certain morale, and move ahead in life, you will definitely achieve your aim.

Dhawal Jaiswal
(Uttar Pradesh)
IPS 2016

Dhawal Jaiswal: I am a resident of Sultanpur, a small town in Uttar Pradesh. I come from a middle class family background. I was only six years old when my father left for heavenly abode. After his death, my uncle has taken care of my family. My success is the result of his hard work. My primary education was done in a local school. I have received my higher education from the Allahabad University, Jawaharlal Nehru University, and University of Delhi. There is a great contribution of these three universities in shaping my personality. Much like most of the youths, I also dreamt of joining a prestigious service, like the Civil

Services. I believe that in this part of our country, the dream of becoming an I.A.S is not our personal dream, rather it becomes the combined dream of a family, a village and a city. For making this dream come true, I had started my journey. In this journey I chose the reading and teaching as my academic career option. I had also worked as an Assistant Professor in the University of Delhi. Keeping in view the uncertainty of success in the Civil Services Examination, choosing an optional career is a positive aspect. By doing so one can become self-dependent and remain free from the unnecessary stress during the examination. I got success in the Civil Services Examination in my fourth attempt. In my previous attempts, I had failed to do a time-management. I had a great difficulty in establishing a balance between the preparations of Civil Services Examination and my academic career.

There are two fundamental mantras for being successful in the Civil Services Examination: patience and continuous hard work. In the present examination system, you cannot adopt an extremely selective view. Studying the whole syllabus is the right strategy. Generally, most of the aspirants remain tense about their family or educational background. Just keep in mind that, this examination tests your ability not your background. Some poet has rightly said-

"Words do not die due to cold,
They die due to lack of courage".

After getting selected in the Civil Services, I only wish to maintain the dignity of my post and discharge my duties as per the provisions under the Constitution of India. In addition, I also want to give my creative contribution in the field of education, which I have gained from my academic experience. I want to give a message to the aspirants of the Civil Services Examination and the youths that they should be confident and focused towards their aim. Try to fix your aims in a phased manner, and try to evaluate from time to time whether you have achieved your aim or not. My special suggestion to the Indian

Languages aspirants is that they must not feel embarrassed on account of their examination medium. Have faith on your yourself and own medium.

Gaurav Singh Sogarwal: I spent my childhood in the agricultural and rural environment on the lands of village Jaghina of Bharatpur district. My father seeded the dream of becoming an I.A.S. in me. Due to my rural background, my attraction towards the Civil Services increased with each passing day. In order to provide a solution to the problem of the common people and to contribute in the nation building, the Civil Services became a mission for me. My family background is associated with a lower middle class rural family. I had a firsthand experience of agriculture and other activities since my childhood. My father was a teacher and my mother is a house wife. We are three siblings. My elder sister had done post-graduation in Zoology and my younger brother is working in a multi-national company in Bangalore after completing his MBA. The dream of joining the Civil Services was seen jointly by me and my father. After the sudden demise of my father in a road accident, my life changed completely. As a result, I saw many ups and downs in my life in the form of family and financial struggle but the dream of joining the Civil Services grew even stronger. After completing my engineering from Pune, I worked for about three years for fulfilling my financial obligations. In the year 2013, I came to Delhi.

Gaurav Singh Sogarwal
(Rajasthan)
IAS 2017

During my struggling days, I faced difficulties in establishing a balance between my studies and family responsibilities. Spiritualism helped me a lot in overcoming it. The regular reading of 'Shrimadbhagvad Gita' and my association with ISCON played the role of a mentor for me.

In my first attempt, I could not clear the prelims exam by just 1 mark; and in my second attempt I failed to pass the mains exam by 2 marks. Though these failures distracted me,but I remembered my initial struggle, and with the help of spiritualism, I decided to do the preparations once again with full dedication and devotion. During this period, I was selected as an Assistant Commandant in BSF.Therefore, the tension of getting an employment got released from my head. In my third attempt, I focused on developing my writing skills for the mains exam and tried to make my weak points stronger.

The newspapers played a pivotal role in my exam strategy. I tried to develop a deep understanding of the incidents happening in my surroundings. I incorporated my background and my experiences in my answers. Consequently, I got more marks in the General Studies than in the Mains exam. For the Essay paper, I did improvements in my time-management and writing-style.

Try to develop an understanding of the incidents happening around you. Try to develop innovative solutions and direct experiences on the issues and incorporate it in your answers. The biographies of great men and spiritualism will be helpful in balancing your personality. Try to accept the ideology of 'Nishkaam Karmayoga'.

Milind Bapna: I am a native of Udaipur (Raj.), a very beautiful city and currently working as a banker. My father is working in a prominent public sector bank and mother is a homemaker and younger sister is a Chartered Accountant(CA).

Milind Bapna
(Rajasthan)
IAS 2017

Initially, I never thought of making a career in civil services, as I always wanted to do an IVY league MBA and enter investment banking/private equity sector but soon I realized that a career as an IAS would give me more diverse options, and most importantly working in a capacity where one can do something for the society and the nation.

I have been working for the past three years as a banker and I managed my studies with my job, although it was tough initially to manage both but with a few sacrifices here and there, it is possible even if you are a working professional.

As I cleared the exam without any sort of coaching, I can firmly say its very possible to be successful with a good strategy and hard work. The current syllabus is more about range rather than depth.So have a wide perspective of issues while reading. Always try to stick to limited resources and revise them well.

Internet can be a great tool during your preparation if used wisely and efficiently.

Mostly, we consider civil services a tough exam to crack, but with my experience I realized it's a fairly moderate exam, only the subjectivity and breadth involved in it makes it look difficult to clear. So if you are motivated and have the right strategy, it is quite achievable.

In my last attempt, I reached interview stage and missed by a whisker (highly disappointing times) and in this attempt I improved on my weak areas and secured a good rank.

So never get disappointed and have faith in yourself and always remember at the end its just another competitive exam and not a test of life.

And always keep other career avenues open, as it will only make you more confident during the entire preparation. I am grateful to my parents, sister, friends etc. for being a constant source of support during my entire journey and my employer who was liberal in giving me leaves for preparation.

Mohammad Mushtaq: I have read in my childhood somewhere that 'Persist and you can change your world', but at that time, these lines were merely words for me. Today I realize that these are not mere words, but these have the capability of changing your life. The story of my success revolves around this persistence to a great extent.

Mohammad Mushtaq
(Bihar)
IPS 2016

I hail from an extremely simple family. I hail from a village in Bihar, where even the facility of electricity is not available. My school education (Matriculation and Intermediate) was done from a government school of my village. I had done my graduation through correspondence from Patna University in the year 2008.

I thought of preparing for the Civil Services since I was studying in Intermediate, but there was no one to guide me. In the beginning phase, my family was worried about me due to the uncertainties of this field. Most of my school friends joined the Indian Air Force, Army and Navy, after passing their matriculation. Therefore in the beginning phase, I also decided to join N.D.A. As I did not know English very well, I failed in P.T itself. In this manner, I tasted the failure in my very first competitive examination.

Failing in NDA examination had made by persistence stronger. I decided that I would do the Civil Services preparations only. In the year 2009, I gave the Preliminary exam of the Civil services at the age of 21, and that too without any preparation of the mains exam. I cleared prelims in my first attempt. Now, I started feeling that I have become a civil servant, but it was my grave mistake. I already knew its result. I failed in the mains exam.

In the year 2010, I improved my preparations and gave my second attempt. This time I cleared the mains exam too. I got good marks in the interview, but I failed to make it in the final merit by a few marks margin. Now I started becoming restless, depressed and tense and this failure broke me.

I received a great shock when in the year 2011, C-SAT was introduced, and I could not clear even the preliminary exam. Now, taking much stress, hopelessness, losing self confidence, sitting alone in the park and talking to myself had become an integral part of my daily routine. My relatives also pressurized me to join some other job.

I could overcome this depression due to the continuous motivation and cooperation of my family, friends and teachers. However, I appeared in CPF Examination, 2011, and got successful in my very first attempt securing the 121st Rank.

The next year, I once again appeared in UPSC examination. This time my preparation was much better than my earlier ones. Finally this time, I got selected for I.R.S. It was quite astonishing. No one, including me, had expected such a success. My persistence, hard work, strong will of not accepting the defeat, the continuous support of my family, the belief of my friends, the blessings of my teachers and good guidance had finally made me a Civil Servant.

However, I still did not lose hope and continuously tried to achieve a better rank. As a result I was once again selected for I.P.S in Civil Services Examination, 2015.

Pradeep Kumar: I was born in a simple middle class family of village Sarad-Alipur, Hisar (Haryana). I passed my matriculation from the village school itself. In those days, there was a great dearth of guidance. The students, who got good marks, used to opt for Science. I did my Intermediate from D.A.V College, Hisar, and then I continued my studies. I did B.Sc., M.Sc., B.Ed., M.Ed. and PhD. Whenever I used to get tired, I heard the sound of my mother's sewing machine and saw my father pressing clothes till 2.am at night after working for the whole day. After completing my M.Ed, I joined as an Assistant Professor in the Saraswati College of Education, Hisar. I was appointed as a Section Officer in the Ministry of Defence in 2011, and as an Inspector in the Income Tax Department in 2012. Due to the inspiration given by my matchless friend Sanjeev, I thought of preparing for the Civil Services.The success of my colleague Ajeet Basant in I.A.S gave me the courage of joining this service, the sole aim of my life.

Pradeep Kumar
(Haryana)
IRS 2015

I believe that devotion, patience and proper guidance play the decisive role in getting success in this exam. In my strategy, the time management has been a major component. Fixing your priorities, and then doing preparations with full discipline, are the basic mantras of being successful in this exam. I have succeeded in clearing this exam in my fourth attempt. When you get success then you fail to know that in which attempt which of the efforts done by you have proved to be helpful. In fact, success is the outcome of cumulative preparations. You learn from your mistakes. It will be better, if you learn from the mistakes committed by others, and by doing so you can minimize the time needed to get success. For youths (especially for UPSC aspirants) some of my brief suggestions are as follows:

1. First of all, prepare a detailed work plan. It should be flexible. For instance, I have to study one subject in the first month and another subject in the second month. Form the habit of reading a good newspaper daily, and try to develop your view on the issues which are more relevant; and write five to six points on the same.

2. In the last week of the month, try to revise the things which you have studied in the whole month. You can also fix any day of the week for doing revision.
3. Keep the exam syllabus in mind and give your full dedication, you will definitely succeed.
4. It is quite natural to face ups and downs during the preparations. Do not pay much attention to it.
5. Make your family your strength. Their support will not let you to get distracted. It will help you in maintaining your focus. In my case, my mother's love, my father's blessings, my brother Sanjay's support, the immense love and care of my wife Neetu and my children Yashika and Sarthak has motivated me in each and every step of my struggle.

Rahul Gupta
(Madhya Pradesh)
IPS 2017

Rahul Gupta: I was born and brought up in Shivpuri, Madhya Pradesh. My father is Sub-engineer in Sarva Siksha Abhiyan in Rajgarh (M.P.). My sister is doing her B.E. from DAVV College, Indore. My mother takes care of all of us.

I have done my schooling from Government School in Shivpuri. Then I cracked JEE from Kota coaching factory by dropping out from school for one year after 12th class. I have done B.Tech. and M.Tech. from IIT Delhi in Electrical Engineering. I completed these degrees in 2014.

I started studying for UPSC CSE in 2013. It was difficult to manage in the beginning because firstly, I decided to take up exam in English medium despite my Hindi medium background till class 12th. So it was difficult to comprehend NCERTs in my first attempt. Secondly, it became very hectic sometimes to manage UPSC preparation and college projects. Coming from engineering background it was difficult to develop genuine interest in the UPSC syllabus and going into the depth.

It came into my mind during penultimate year of the college because career path had to be chosen. I realized that I will remain happy in life if I am able to see tangible impact of my work. Additionally, I wanted a job where commonsense application rather than theoretical knowledge is applied. Thus I found civil services as the best career option at that time.

I failed to clear mains stage in first attempt. It was definitely a setback. But on honest introspection I found that there were some areas where I was unprepared and I needed greater effort in next attempt if I had to clear this exam, which I did with greater amount of hard work in the second attempt.

I have appeared for CSE 3 times. In second attempt I got 306th rank, in third 182nd rank.

Book list is common for 90 percent of candidates who clear this exam. Anyone can find them of blogs of selected candidates. But what is more important is understanding of the syllabus and its application in real life. Questions being asked are very dynamic and current affairs related, so one has to be thorough with them. Answer writing skills are becoming very important these days as weightage to general studies has increased. Moreover, consistent hard work is needed. Choose your optional subject wisely because one has to be master of it, so genuine interest is needed.

Do what you feel will make you happy, because then only one can attain excellence and live a happy life. Try choose your career path because of your parents' or society's expectations. Be the master of your own destiny, carve out your own path. Failures are part of life. Remember Edison failed 1000 times before inventing the electric bulb.

Rajat Saklecha: Whoever has seen the bollywood movie 'Jab We Met' will be acquainted with my home town Ratlam. Although it is a film and the town's description has been portrayed in a filmic manner. The real Ratlam is famous for namkeens and designer jewellery of pure gold in the whole country. I have done my schooling from this town. My father works in the State Bank of India in Ratlam. The other members of my family are my mother, elder brother and grandparents. The boys who get birth in small towns are also treated as other's wealth and they leave their homes one day or the other for studying and achieving something in life. I did my Civil Engineering from Indore and came to Delhi for fulfilling my childhood dream of joining the Civil Services. I started appearing in the Civil Services Examination in the year 2012. In my first attempt, I cleared prelims only; in my second attempt I cleared both the prelims and mains exam; and finally in my third attempt, I was selected as an I.P.S.

Rajat Saklecha
(Madya Pradesh)
IPS 2016

I had seen the dream of joining the Civil Services in my childhood itself. There were many reasons behind it. The most important factor was my habit of reading newspapers since childhood. Reading newspapers helped me in gathering general knowledge about my town, country and the world. When I faced various difficulties in day- to- day life, then I realized that to do something for my family and for the society, joining the Civil Services is the best option..

To be successful, you need not only work hard, but there are several other motivating factors which help you in achieving the success. Besides fate, the continuous support of my family and friends, the spirit of never losing hope and working more hard for getting success are the factors which have helped me in attaining the success and becoming a Civil Servant. The most important thing for doing the Civil Services Examination preparations is your knowledge and analytical view on the events happening around you. The daily newspapers, some weekly magazines, Wikipedia,

Quora website and Google are very helpful for acquiring the knowledge. Besides, for presenting your knowledge in a better way, you can write your answers on the websites like insightsonindia and IASbaba etc. I have done most of my studies online, because the coaching notes appeared cumbersome to me. If you read some notes thoroughly, then it saves your precious time. In short, do not study the same topic from various sources and keep revising the things which you have studied earlier.

I believe that if you study sincerely for 7-8 hours then it is more than sufficient. Sometimes you can study in a light manner, but the continuity must be maintained. If you want to achieve something, find meaning in life and make efforts for the society's betterment by achieving something. If your aim is noble, there is honesty in your efforts and you are moving in the right direction, then you will definitely get success. In today's era, when everything is available on the internet,it is you who can stop yourself from being successful, otherwise the world it at your disposal.

Sagar Bagmar: Myself, Sagar Bagmar, from Balotra, Barmer (Rajasthan). I have completed my B.Com. from Satyawati College, Delhi University in 2013. I am from a middle class family and my father is in Textile Business. I have completed my schooling from Balotra.

Sagar Bagmar
(Rajasthan)
IPS 2017

Coming from small town was always a challenge to get good education yet I tried to get good sources for quality education which was supported by my teachers and friends.

Thought for appearing in CSE started developing when I came to know about the public welfare works done by my two inspirational personalities Sh. L. K. Panwar Sir (IAS) and Sh. JasrajJi Chopra (Retd. Justice).

Failures are part and parcel of life. So rather than getting disappointed we should try to correct our mistakes and maintain self-confidence along with positive attitude towards life. That's what I followed when I couldn't clear CSE in first attempt. In second attempt, I cleared CSE 2015 with AIR 454 and got into IRS (C&CE) and CSE 2016 with AIR 186.

After completing my graduation in 2013 I started preparing for UPSC CSE and didn't opted for any job. Total, I have given 3 attempts to CSE.

CSE preparation requires "Right Material, Right Guidance, More Revision, More Writing Practice ". I always tried to study minimum source for a topic and not too many books for same topic. Self notes preparation from newspaper helped me a lot. Aspirant should always focus on reading one newspaper.

We, the Youth, are the future of this country. I remember a beautiful quote,

"*Stop looking to others, and be Your Own Hero. Be the best of you that you can be*".

Shashank Tripathi: I grew up in Kanpur. I received my education till Class XII from the Jugal Devi Saraswati Vidya Mandir. My father Shri Shrinarayana Tripathi works as an Office Superintendent in this School itself. My mother Suman Tripathi is a homemaker. My parents were fully devoted to the idea that they would let their children do their studies irrespective of the hardships they would face in doing so. After passing the intermediate, I did Chemical Engineering from IIT, Kanpur.

Shashank Tripathi
(Uttar Pradesh)
IAS 2016

My struggle is the struggle of a Hindi medium student. I had done my schooling in Hindi medium and had studied in IIT in English medium. I have realized in Class X itself that, although Hindi is my strength, but if I remain weak in English, then it will pose problems for me. From that time I started focusing on English too. This story continued in UPSC too, where I had written the Sanskrit literature paper in English medium. After working in college Placement Cell, I came to know about various jobs. Then, I decided to join the Civil Services. In the final year of my college itself, I had decided that I would do the Civil Services preparations. Therefore, I did not sit in the campus placement, and instead I focused on my preparations.

I gave my first attempt in the year 2014. I got 272nd rank and was allotted I.R.S (Income-Tax). In my second attempt in 2015, I got 5th rank and was allotted I.AS in the Uttar Pradesh cadre.

Maintaining this motivation level was the most important thing for me. Right motivation provided me the strength for doing both hard and smart work. On one hand, I studied very deeply for my optional subject, on the other hand I did a general level preparation of General Studies by studying the basic books. I prepared the Current Affairs very well. It is very important to join a test series and solve the previous year question papers. I had practiced writing essays too. Taking Sanskrit Literature as my optional subject was a very important decision of my life. After getting success, now my strongest desire is to become an able and honest officer. I will try my level best to fulfill my duties under the guidance of my senior officers.

Swati Kumari Sujata: Success is not a destination, instead it is the path which is full of challenges,meaning a continuously changing and moving life.The desire of becoming its traveler resides in human beings only. In fact, even I do not exactly know how much distance have I covered in this path, but after getting selected in Civil

Services, I have certainly experienced that at least I have done an honest attempt to move my step forward in life's path.

I basically hail from Patna, Bihar. My father is an Engineer. The suggestion and cooperation given to me by my parents and brother since my childhood had motivated me to join the Civil Services. Gradually I came to understand the importance of the Civil Services and the pivotal role it plays in the development of society. Since the time of Engineering Final Year, I had decided my future course of action. I was selected as an IT Manager in my field, i.e., Engineering, but I did not join it and started preparing for UPSC Civil Services.

Swati Kumari Sujata
(Bihar)
IRS 2015

In the same year in 2011, I got married. My husband works in the Bihar Administrative Services. After my marriage, I continued my preparations by maintaining a balance and coordination between my family responsibilities and personal expectations. My husband and his whole family supported my decision, and they kept motivating me. It was the result of the love and support, which I had received from my family, that I did not lose hope even after failing in the prelims exam in my initial two attempts. For gaining confidence, I also appeared in various other competitive examinations. I was also selected as an Assistant Manager in the Bank of India, and as a Management Trainee in the Food Corporation of India. After joining this job too, I continued my Civil Services Examination preparations. My optional subject was Hindi Literature and my medium was Hindi. Although the study materials in Hindi for UPSC competition is comparatively less available; but the proper guidance provided by different institutions and teachers in Delhi, and doing a self study along with the time management helped me in overcoming this problem. Every subject was new for me. Therefore, in my strategy I gave preference to doing a continuous writing practice. Preparing for Civil Services Examination gave me a new humane view by dint of which I was able to analyze the things happening in the society from a fresh perspective and without any traditional predetermined and biased lens.

In UPSC Civil Services Examination, 2015 I got 796th rank and was allotted I.R.S. This result made me familiar with my limitations and strengths. I believe that we all are capable of achieving something great in life. The only thing, which is required to achieve success, is to use that capacity in a proper and honest way. My success in UPSC is not only the identity given to me by my rank, but my identity lies in a greater task, i.e., to work responsibly towards the nation's interests which can be attained only through following the values of serving humanity. The power of doing self-introspection is the best gift which I have received from the Civil Services Exam.

Sachin Jain
(Uttar Pradesh)
IRS 2016

Sachin Jain: In UPSC Civil Services Examination, 2015 I got 286th rank and was allotted I.R.S. I am a resident of a town Baraut,situated in Western Uttar Pradesh. My father is an Accountant and my mother is a homemaker. I had done my schooling in the Hindi medium from my home town. I was always very good in mathematics from my school days; hence I got admission in Engineering in Lucknow. However, I faced many challenges there especially in learning English and Computer. Those were the days of joy, when I remained tensionfree and enjoyed with my friends. I got a job in Wipro, Hyderabad through campus placement, but the work pressure was too much there. During this period

I thought that if I can work so hard then, I should try for India's best job.

Thereafter, I left my job and came to Delhi to do the Civil Services preparations. I cleared P.T in my very first attempt, and then I realized that I have reached the seventh heaven; but then began the series of my failures,i.e., I failed in the four consecutive mains exam and all my four attempts were finished. Fortunately, after two attempts I got a job in the United India Insurance Company, Indore. In this job I got enough time to study and the financial problem was also solved. Besides, I also started teaching the Civil Services aspirants in morning and in evening. While giving coaching, I made good notes of all the best books. Finally the news came that the government had decided to increase two more attempts for appearing in the Civil Services. After hearing this news, I instantly stopped teaching and took leave from my job and came to Delhi once again. This time my efforts bore fruit and in UPSC, 2014, I got 714th rank. I did not lose hope even then, and in my last attempt I got 286th rank. This journey of mine was full of difficulties, but it taught me many things.

I want to say to the Civil Services Examination aspirants that you should read the standard books of UPSC for at least three times and should do the writing practice daily. Do not waste your time in thinking about which coaching is the best, which book is the best, which website is the best and which effort is the best. You should research about these things in the very beginning of your preparations and then you should start preparing for your Optional Subject. Try to make notes daily before going to sleep. Stop thinking and start working. If you make efforts honestly, then believe that you will get success for sure.

Shailendra Bamania: My father is a Lecturer of Botany in the Government Post-Graduate College, Karauli (Rajasthan), and my mother is a homemaker. I have four siblings, i.e., two elder sisters, one younger brother, and I am the third child of my parents. I have received my education till M.Sc. in Karauli district from the Hindi medium, hence I never paid attention to English's utility. After passing Class XII, I started studying English for the Civil Services preparations. During my studies, I never faced any economic problems as my father was in government service. During graduation, my father motivated me to choose the Civil Services as a career. Therefore after graduation, I did M.A. in Public Administration, because then it was the most popular subject in the Civil Services. As I had to select two optional subjects, I did M.Sc. in Botany too.

Shailendra Bamania
(Rajasthan)
IPS 2016

Keeping in mind the uncertainty of getting success in Civil Services Examination, I gave NET in both the subjects so that an option of becoming a Lecturer was always there for me. Besides, I also kept appearing in SSC, Bank and RPSC examinations. I also got selected in these exams. In addition, the most important thing was that I motivated myself during the times of my failures and said to myself that I have the capability of clearing the Civil Services Examination and I can do it. My parents and siblings always motivated me and they never let me leave hope during the times of my failures. This was my seventh attempt in Civil Services Examination. Prior to this, I had given mains exams in 2009, 2010, 2012, 2013, and 2014. I had appeared in the interview in 2012 and I failed in the prelims exam itself in the year 2011.

I had selected Botany and Public Administration as my optional subjects from 2009 to 2012. In 2012, new exam pattern was introduced by UPSC and I selected Public Administration as my optional subject in 2013 and 2014,but I did not perform well in the Public Administration,therefore in the year 2015, I selected Botany as my optional subject and obtained 249 marks. Although I knew that I have a good command over Botany, but somewhere in my mind I thought that the subject like Botany is meant only for the English medium aspirants, which was the biggest mistake. This year I selected Botany as my optional subject in place of Public Administration and became successful.

As no coaching or notes and books of Botany in Hindi are available for doing the Civil Services preparations, therefore, I started making notes by myself from the Hindi medium books of graduation level;but only 30-40 percent of syllabus could be covered from it.Therefore, for studying the rest of topics, I did an online search and whatever I got from the search, I translated it in Hindi and made notes. Besides, I also purchased the study notes of Evolution Coaching in Mukherjee Nagar and I prepared rest of the topics by doing its Hindi Translation. During my preparations, my father who is a lecturer of Botany helped me a lot.

In this manner for doing the last time revision, I made brief notes of Botany in Hindi, comprising only three registers, so that I can do my overall preparations during the exam in much less time. These brief notes played a pivotal role in making me successful.

Vivek Kumar Yadav: My father Sonelal Yadav is a Physiotherapist Technician in the Department of Medicine, Uttar Pradesh. I am the youngest among my three brothers. My elder brother Santosh Kumar Yadav works as a Software Engineer, while my younger brother Sandeep Kumar Yadav is posted in Department of Posts.

Vivek Kumar Yadav
(Uttar Pradesh)
PCS 2014

The blessing 'May you study well and become an officer'!, received from my elders since my childhood, and getting the opportunity of receiving prizes from the I.A.S officers on various occasions during my school days, made me realize the prestige, dignity and importance of this post. Therefore, I saw the dream of making a career in the Civil Services from my school days itself. My parents gave strength to my desires and my family gave me emotional support. In 2013, I expressed my desire in front of my family that I wanted to do Civil Services Examination preparations.

With the blessings of my family and God, I got selected and achieved 1st rank in my very first attempt of UPPCS, 2013. For doing the Civil Services preparations, I personally believe that an aspirant should fix his/her target that how much he/she has to study daily, keeping in mind the previous year question papers and the exam syllabus. If you fix the achievable target, then not only will you get success but also your struggle will end in the stipulated time.

Never shun the tendency of positive thinking, self-confidence and self-introspection during your preparations. It will help you from time to time in making your strategy well planned and determined. If you are able to develop the understanding that what you have to study and what you need not to study, then you can manage your time easily. A few hours of regular studies and revision can improve both your time management and self confidence. While doing your preparations you can make your preparation multidimensional, complete and balanced by taking help of the standard books, newspapers, and magazines. In addition, you can also take the help of internet, tips from the successful aspirants and especially from the websites and educational video lectures available on the internet for the Civil Services Examination preparations. Keeping in mind the recent trend, developing a good understanding of Current Affairs and incorporating your multidimensional view in your answers will help you in obtaining good marks.

While doing the Civil Services Examination preparations, have full faith on your capacities and abilities. Keep your target in mind and try to work towards achieving it with full honesty and dedication.

Do not get scared of your failures and maintain your self confidence. Always keep this in mind and play games, give time to your hobbies and fulfill your social responsibilities. The only thing needed to get success is honesty and persistence in your studies.

❑❑

16

The Story of My Success

"When you want to achieve something desperately, you move ahead by following the signs which you get from time to time; then the whole universe holds your hands to help you ". I feel that this message of Paulo Coelho's famous book 'Alchemist' suits very well on the untold story of my struggle and success.

I came out from a small lane of an old city area of Meerut in Uttar Pradesh, and I have been able to make my dream true which I saw in my childhood by moving ahead on the path of success gradually and step by step; but sometimes I feel that the journey of my success has been like a dream.

I have never written anything about myself. After contemplating a lot, I am trying to gather enough courage to write about me. I will try to share with you some light-heavy burdens, pains, expectations, pleasures and smiles, which are hidden somewhere in the soft corner of my heart.

I was born in a simple family, living in a lane of an old city. My grandfather worked as a Junior Court Officer in the court. He was an extremely honest person. He used to pack his food from home and used to walk to his work place on foot and came back home on foot. My grandmother was not much educated but she very well knew the importance of education and knowledge. My father was second among his four brothers. In short, I grew up in a simple middle class family. My father had somehow studied till Class X, and my mother was a graduate of her times. Hence, much emphasis was laid on studies at my home.

It is the story of those days when I used to study in Class 8th or 9th. We used to go to buy groceries at the Government PDS Grocery Shop. The shopkeeper often remained absent. We used to hear his made-up stories. I read our yellow ration-card and in the card's bottom it was written: 'Food and Supplies Officer'. I thought that if these irregularities and deformities can be corrected by becoming an officer then I too will become an officer. I told this to my parents, but none paid heed to my desire.

At that time Shri Awnish Awasthi was the Collector of Meerut. I was fond of reading the newspapers in those days too. I read daily in the newspaper about the good things being done by the Collector. My young mind was deeply impressed by the initiatives, improvements and work done by him. Now I thought deep in my heart that I would have to become a Collector. My elder brother told me that in order to become a Collector, you would have to pass I.A.S examination,which is extremely tough. Fortunately, I was good at studies and I was very interested in taking part in the co-curricular activities, like debate, essay, quiz, poetry recitation etc. My elder brother told me that if you wished to become an I.A.S officer, then you should move ahead with your dream.

In fact, I passed my Intermediate in Commerce stream from a Government Inter College. Fortunately, I got the highest marks in my district. Although I liked the science and commerce, but was naturally interested in the subjects of humanities, like social science and language and literature. On the other hand my dream of doing UPSC preparations was also getting stronger, and it was the prevalent notion during those days, that the students of Arts stream perform very well in UPSC. On one hand, all my friends were filling the form of C.A. (Chartered Accountant), while on the other hand I and two of my other friends decided to do B.A. from the Meerut College. We did not think about taking admission in Delhi or Allahabad University, because residing and studying outside home was a costly affair.

In this manner, I did graduation with history, political science and English literature. The days of Meerut College are very memorable. I remained very busy in my studies and extracurricular activities. During graduation, I took part in dozens of debate, essay, poetry recitation, quiz competitions of National and State level, and got first prize in most of them. I also took very active part in N.C.C and N.S.S. I still remember that during a National Social Service camp, we collected the unused medicines by going door to door for the people who really needed them. The national organization of youths, like N.C.C and N.S.S definitely strengthen the national integrity, discipline, *esprit de corps* and social concern. I was the regular student editor of the Meerut College's magazine. Apart from this, I secured a position in the University's merit list also.

I never forget my teachers of Meerut College, especially the then Principal Dr. S. K. Aggarwal and Dr. Ramyagya Maurya, Lecturer, Department of Hindi. Although Hindi, Sanskrit, Urdu and Philosophy were not my subjects in graduation, but due to my interest in these subjects, I often visited these departments. To find a dedicated and humble person like Principal Sir is very rare. One can learn the art of giving positive motivation from him. When I and my friends returned to the college after winning the first prize and shield in the debate competition, the Principal Sir not only appreciated us but also distributed sweets to all the staff members and he bore its expenses from his own pocket.

My dreams were big, but there were some economic problems too. I remember that I and my two other friends used to do some part time jobs of reading and writing after doing the matriculation itself. For instance, I did the proof reading of books and creative writing. These small part time jobs taught some big lessons of life. I never forget a major and an interesting incident, which happened during my post- graduation, and sometimes I feel that this incident has become the turning point of my life. There was a senior of mine who was very kind hearted. He always used to motivate me. Once he said to me, "If a light bulb is kept near the ground of a room then how much light it will give, and if the same light bulb is hung on the roof then how much light it will give". His hint was very clear; if you possess the capability of contributing to society after attaining a high level. then you should definitely give it a try.

I started preparing for UGC NET-JRF Examination in Hindi Literature, and fortunately I cracked it in my first attempt. Besides, I also gave M.Phil. Entrance examinations of the University of Delhi and JNU and qualified both the exams. I took admission in D.U., and finally reached Delhi with the hope of making my dreams true. I used to feel nostalgic and homesick. Although late, but still I had left home for the first time in my life for doing my studies (although Meerut is not very far off from Delhi). I still remember that I had written a poem titled, **'A Message to My Mother'** while I was missing my home and my mother very badly. I am sharing the poem with you as most of my aspirant friends will be able to associate themselves with the English version of my poem:

"You are a unique treasure of feelings;
you are an ocean of desires,
You are like a soft cover of tender feelings.

Some harsh and some lovely scolding
and then loving back in return,
Every moment of my life is because of you,

and the whole world is because of you.

You have sacrificed everything for me,
even your pleasures,
But your son does not have enough time
to wipe you tears.

When I move towards the big city
to fulfill my desire,
I saw you crying from within and
I came to know what true love is.

You are the sweet smell of the soil
and soft wetness of relations,
In a new city I achieved new heights
but I really missed you.

I wonder every face in the city
wore many masks and veils,
But there was no one like you
as you are an open book of life.

You are the warmth of relations;
you are the feeling of love,
You were always there with me
in the form of my prayers.

Who says that one cannot see
angels in this world?
Once you sleep in your mother's lap,
all your dreams are fulfilled ".

I feel that I have learnt so much during one and a half year period spent the University of Delhi. From the academic environment of University of Delhi.

At the same time, in the year 2013 I appeared in the Civil Services Prelims Exam of the Union public Service Commission as well as in the PCS prelims exam of my home state Uttar Pradesh. My preparations were good and my motivation level was also very high. Till today, I had passed each and every academic and competitive examination with good marks,but this time, something else had happened. I failed in both the exams by a margin of 2 to 5 marks. Perhaps for the first time in my life, I had tasted failure. For some time, I felt that all my dreams were shattered. I was losing hope and started feeling depressed. Perhaps I was unable to handle my failure. This was the most difficult phase of my journey.

Confusion was increasing continuously and I was feeling that my career had gone into doldrums. In those days, one day I wrote the following poem in Hindi titled, 'I am a city', which was later published in the magazine, 'Kadambini':

'I am a city...
Carrying the burdens of smiles,
Busy in my own world,
I look for some time,
I am a city.

In the seamless crowd,
I do not guard the shadows,
I run continuously,
I do not know when the evening comes
and when the dawn comes,
I am a city.

In the market of dreams,
How beautiful are the artificial smiles,
Eyes in the eyes, conversations in the conversations,
Like a gap in closeness,
I am a city.

In the soft chamber of my heart,
I am carrying such a huge burden,
Perhaps it has been quite some time,
When I enjoyed playing with paper boats.
I am all over my own emotions,
Whether I am a comfort or a curse,
I am a city'.

But in these hard times, my family, especially my elder brother Prashant Jain and some of my friends, appeared before me like the life savers. They gave me emotional support and also encouraged me. I can say that my family and well wishers had more confidence in me than I had in myself. I gathered some courage and on the other side, I heard the news of my success in another examination

(Translator in Lok Sabha Secretariat). After submitting my M.Phil. dissertation, I joined this job in Parliament House.

This job not only taught me many things but also increased my confidence. Along with it, I became tensionfree about my career. I feel that despite of the business of this job, it helped me in doing UPSC preparations without any tension and pressure; it also helped me in writing my exams in a calm manner. In 2014, I once again gave the prelims exam of both UPSC and UPPCS. This time fate supported me, and I passed in the prelims exam of both UPSC and UPPCS. This time I was not prepared to take any risk, therefore, despite of the fact that there was a gap of only one month between the mains exams of UPSC and State Public Service Commission, I appeared in both the exams. This time very few people knew that I was appearing in both the mains exams. I was totally satisfied after giving both the mains exam, and I was almost certain of my success. This time I had followed all the three guiding principles of my life, i.e., Nishkaam Karmayoga (Geeta), Anekantavad (Jain Philosphy), and Middle Path (Buddhist Philosphy) and gave my examinations with full concentration.

I got the interview call from UPSC. In the interview board of Prof. H.C. Gupta, my interview continued for about thirty five minutes. During the interview and after the interview too, my mind was calm and cool. On the other side, the result of UPPCS Mains was still pending; therefore, I appeared in the prelims exam of UPPCS, 2015 which I had qualified too.

Now I was eagerly waiting for my result. To be on the verge of the final selection gives a different feeling altogether. Sometimes I used to get scared by thinking that if I do not get finally selected then what will happen to me. Will my life really change one day? Such questions and confusions continuously came in my mind,but I always pacified my mind by saying that I had failed to pass even the prelims exam in my previous attempt. This time I had appeared in the interview, it is an achievement, and I need not to worry as I already have a job.

It was a sunny afternoon of 3rd July, 2015. I had gone to Allahabad to appear in the mains exam of UPPCS. However, I had got the interview call for the previous year's PCS examination. After visiting Sangam, when I returned back to Delhi, I came to know that tomorrow, i.e., on 4th July the final result of UPSC Civil Services Examination is going to be declared. As it was a weekend, I decided to go to Meerut and see my result at home. I took a bus in the morning from Anand Vihar Bus Terminal for Meerut and reached home. In the afternoon, I came to know that the result is going to be announced any moment now. My family was more nervous than me. Around One o'clock I got a phone call, and I was told that I had got the 13th rank and had got first rank from the Hindi medium. Thereafter, wishes started pouring in. Later on, when I saw the mark sheet, I came to know that I have got the third highest marks (851 marks) in the mains exam. Besides, I got 160 marks in the Essay and 313 marks in the Optional Subject which is possibly the highest obtained mark in these papers till date. I got 124 marks in the Ethics paper too and I got total 378 marks in the General studies. My overall marks were 1001 which was nothing less than a good omen for me.

Success brings with itself many expectations and responsibilities. Out of these things, one thing is very important – the handling of your success. Many of our friends change their behavior after getting small success; or sometimes, we get over excited due to our happiness. Success demands a little bit maturity and sincerity. I am satisfied with the fact that the honour and identity which I got after this success was handled very well by me with the help of my family, friends and teachers and I normally remained in my natural state.

During this period I received many honours, and I got the opportunity to give the motivational talks to youths and aspirants on various occasions. The biggest day of my life was the day when my felicitation ceremony was graced with the presence of Hon. Lok Sabha Speaker Mrs. Sumitra Mahajan ji in the Parliament House's Convention Centre. In the convention centre, all the officers and staff of Lok Sabha Secretariat were present with whom I was working for the last two years. I feel that this honour was not my honour as an individual person,instead it was the honour given to the achievement of an aspirant who came from a normal background.

Today when I recall these golden memories,then sometimes, I feel that many things have changed but sometimes I feel that nothing has changed at all. The only thing that has changed is that I will not have to fill forms again for the employment. My family has become tensionfree about my career, and naturally there has been a certain uplift in my social status; but there are certain things which has not changed and I wish that they may not change i.e., the desire of continuously moving ahead and doing something better in life, remaining continuously progressive, doing continuous hard work and trying my level best to face the new challenges.

I feel that I got a high rank in UPSC because of the three factors: my accumulated knowledge and experience, my writing skill and my comprehensive and balanced view. Besides, I also feel that my every job, every educational institution, every teacher and every friend has taught me so many things. My friends used to say that, 'My preparation was silent, but my success was stupendous'.

Really, success is not a destination, it is the beginning of a new journey instead. A poet has given the same expression in the following manner:

"Whether I get my destination or not,
I do not give it a care,
I am satisfied with the fact that
I am in the Caravan searching its destination".

I just want to say that, wherever you are, however you live, whatever you do, do it happily, keep yourself engaged and keep enjoying. Do not lose hope by listening to the words of a pessimistic person. At last I would like to share the following four lines of Dushyant Kumar, a renowned Hindi poet, which have always motivated me in the journey of my struggle:

SUNDAY TI

Bennett, Coleman & Co. Ltd.

JULY 5, 2015 | MEERUT | PAGES 32 | INCLUDING TIMESLIFE! AND MEERUT TIMES | TIMESOFINDIA.COM | EPAPER.TIMESOFINDIA

OF INDIA

TIMES CITY

SUNDAY TIMES OF INDIA, NEW DELHI / MEERUT
JULY 5, 2015

City lad 13th in UPSC, 1st in Hindi medium

Pankul Sharma | TNN

Meerut: Nishant Jain, a 28-year-old, has done the city proud, securing the 13th rank at the all-India level in the UPSC's civil services examination and topping in the Hindi medium.

Jain's preparation for one of the country's toughest and most prestigious examinations was no less arduous. Jain completed his masters in Hindi from Meerut College and MPhil from Delhi University. He then joined the Lok Sabha secretariat as Hindi assistant.

"After joining the Lok Sabha secretariat, I set the goal of clearing UPSC for myself. In my first attempt I couldn't clear the preliminary but I never gave up and went for the second attempt," said Jain, who also relied, for spiritual support, on the teachings of Mahaveer.

"It is said in the Tattvartha Sutra that living beings benefit by helping each other. So I did not ignore any person I knew whose presence was of help to me. I also kept it in mind that time and energy are both limited and they must not be wasted," he added.

He expressed the hope that his performance, particularly topping in Hindi medium, would encourage those from a Hindi background. "Particularly aspirants from a small city like Meerut. It doesn't matter what subject we choose, we have to have confidence in our choice and must know the subject," Jain added.

Youngest of three siblings, Jain's eldest brother, Prashant, is a journalist with the Times Group, while his elder sister is a government employee. Nishant completed his schooling from Saraswati Shishu Mandir and K K Inter College at Meerut. During his college days, he was student editor of Meerut College's official magazine, 'Abhivyakti', and was also a member of its literary and cultural council. Jain is a prolific writer, with a number of poems and articles published in newspapers and magazines.

The civil services examination is conducted by the UPSC annually in three stages — preliminary, mains and interviews — to select candidates for the elite Indian Administrative Service (IAS), Indian Foreign Service (IFS) and Indian Police Service (IPS), among others.

Manish Kumar

Nishant Jain

"After joining the Lok Sabha secretariat, I set the goal of clearing UPSC for myself. In my first attempt I couldn't clear the preliminary but I never gave up and went for the second attempt

NISHANT JAIN
Hindi medium Topper

"The cold breeze does come from the current of this river,
Although the boat is feeble, but it challenges the waves.
Go and find a spark from somewhere my friends,
There is still some zeal left in you, try to light it".

❑❑

Appendix

A Glimpse of Training: The Foundation Course

Finally, that day arrived which I had dreamt of since my young age,i.e., the big day of the training's beginning at the Lal Bahadur Shastri National Academy of Administration, Mussoorie (LBSNAA), known as 'The Destination of Dreams'. This much awaited training was scheduled to begin on the 7th September, 2015.

I, along with my family members, reached Mussoorie, 'the Queen of the Hills', on the afternoon of 6th September, 2015. Incidentally, I came to Mussoorie for the first time. My heart started beating fast, as we proceeded from the Mussoorie's Library Point, thinking about the academy of dreams and about the colleagues and the environment there.

With a pounding heart, I entered the Academy's gate. After entering the academy, I realized that the academy, though appeared very small from the outside, was very big and splendid from inside. I can not express the Academy's beauty in words. It is wonderful and incredible. Situated in the lap of nature, it appears to be the example of a marvelous architecture. Interestingly, the buildings inside the Academy have been named as Karmashila, Gyanshila, Dhruvshila and Aadharshila, and the hostels have been named on the names of the rivers, like Narmada, Ganga and Kaveri.

A room in the Kaveri hostel was allotted to me. As I was moving towards the hostel with my luggage, a colleague enquired about the Kaveri hostel's location. As soon as I reached my room, the door bell rang. I opened the door to find out that the same colleague was my roommate. He hailed from Kerala, and was allotted the Indian Revenue Service. All the newly selected officers, participating in the academy's Foundation course, are addressed as the Officer Trainee (O.T).

The training at the Mussoorie Academy began with the Foundation Course. Ours was the '90th Foundation Course'. It is an entry level course, mandatory for the Officer Trainees of various Civil Services of India, like I.A.S,I.F.S,I.P.S,I.R.S etc. The duration of this course is generally three months and a week.

The Foundation course, as evident from its name, is a basic course meant for developing the desired skills, knowledge and aptitude in the new entrant young officers of the academy. It aims to make the Officer Trainees aware of the administrative, social, economic and political environment of the country, to develop the feeling of mutual support and co-ordination among the trainees of the various Civil Services, and thus develop their overall personality. In this course, the emphasis is given on the *'esprit de corps'*, which means developing the spirit of solidarity among the young officers hailing from the various regions, religions, linguistic, social, economic and tribal backgrounds of a multilingual country India, so that they can relate themselves with one another and feel associated.

Well, returning to the date of 7th September'2015, i.e., the first day of the training, our day began at 6 o'clock in the morning. About 350 young officers gathered at the Polo Ground for P.T.Every day, we used to reach at the fixed time for P.T after crossing the high and low hilly roads. We used to do the physical exercise for about 45 minutes in a lovely cold weather, and return back to our hostels. The academic classes used to begin at 9 o'clock in the morning. Since today was the opening ceremony of the 90th Foundation Course,it was mandatory for us to wear the ceremonial dress,i.e., the Jodhpuri Bandgala suit for males and Saree for females. The Officer Trainees looked immensely attractive in this dress.

The opening ceremony was devoted to the course of briefing and ice breaking. Shri Sanjay Kothari, Secretary, Department of Personnel and Training, Government of India, was the chief guest of the ceremony. During the ceremony, the academy's song 'Hao Dharmete Dhir, Hao Karmete Bir, Hao Unnat Shir' was sung in full throated voice, and we were made to remember the ideal message of the sentence inscribed in the academy's logo: 'Shilam param Bhushnam'.

In the evening, various interesting ice breaking sessions were conducted to break the barriers in the dialogue through various activities and games so that everyone gets a chance to know one another and get acquainted.

Second day onwards, the classes formally starteddaily at 9 o'clock after our morning P.T. session. After the P.T.sessions, we used to get ready in our formal dress and go for the breakfast at the Officers' Mess. Despite of all the time management, we always used to reach the classes by running hard.

On the second day, the 'course briefing' was done,i.e., a detailed information about the dimensions of the foundation course as well as the academic and co-curricular activities was given. Here, I would like to share the gist of the briefing sessions with you. The classes were organized from morning till evening. In the foundation course's academic inputs, mainly six subjects were taught. The faculty members and the experts, comprising the professors and senior officers of the various Civil Services and the guest speakers, comprising the senior public representatives and officers, administrators, professors, scholars and social personalities, were also invited from outside the academy to guide us.

The major subject areas taught in the foundation course are:

1. Public Administration
2. Economics
3. Law
4. Management
5. Political Thought and the Constitution of India
6. Indian History and Culture.

The area of the above mentioned subjects is generally very broad, hence the academy lays much emphasis on those aspects which are extremely important from the point of view of administration.

Apart from the above six subjects, two more subjects are also taught: Information and Communication Technology (ICT) and Language. In the Language subject, one has to select one language out of the 22 Indian Languages offered in the syllabus. For instance, I decided to learn Urdu. I will discuss my experience of learning the Urdu language later on.

Besides the academic inputs in the foundation course, we are supposed to write two major assignments: Essay and Book Review, and submit it within the stipulated time. We used to write the essays on the immensely varied subjects, like national security, national integrity and communal harmony, human rights and scientific and human development etc., and review the non-fiction books.

The co-curricular activities, like trekking, horse riding, village visit, cultural activities, various creative activities of the clubs and societies, Shramdan and blood donation camps etc. organized in the academy, fill the academy with vibrant colors. These interesting activities save the Officer Trainees from the training's monotony as well as develop their overall personality by making them mingle and interact with one another. These co-curricular activities are evaluated and various medals and prizes are distributed to the best performers accordingly.

The pace of our life in the academy gradually began to hot up. The academic classes were in full swing, andit was mandatory for us to attend the classes regularly and on time.

Apart from the academic classes, one more input was given to us in the first week of our training,i.e., Extra Curricular Module (E.C.M). In order to ensure the participation of every Officer Trainee in the co-curricular activities, they were asked to choose one E.C.M., which included badminton, tennis, billiards, music, singing and playing instruments, painting, photography, cooking, baking, horse riding etc. Separate sessions were organized to teach the above modules.

In the very first week, another interesting activity - the election of the academy's various clubs and societies was organized. These unique societies include the Film Society, Fine Arts Association, Hobbies Club, House Journal Society (Literary Club), Management Circle, Nature Lovers Club, Officers' Club, Officers' Mess, Social Service Society, Rifle and Archery Club, and Contemporary Affairs Society etc. These clubs/societies provide the officer trainees a unique opportunity to work in their own areas of interest and learn something new.

These Officer Trainees elect the Secretary and the members of these societies from among their own batch of the officer trainees. After filing the nominations, they are provided with the opportunity to campaign for their candidature. For campaigning, all the candidates are given the opportunity to put forward the reasons before all the Officer Trainees as to why they should be elected. I was nominated for the Secretary, Literary Club of the academy, i.e., 'House Journal Society'; and after the online voting, I got elected.

By the end of the first week of our training, our weekly trekking activity began.The trekking experience was interesting and unique in many aspects, as the trekking through the zigzag, narrow and high-low paths amidst wonderful natural splendor filled us with thrills. There are lovely, famous and beautiful treks in Mussoorie. Short treks from the academy to Kempty Falls, Binog Hills and Lal Tibba were organized on every weekend in the first three weeks of our stay in Mussoorie.

I second the opinion of the people in the academy that an Officer Trainee never forgets the experience and emotions of trekking in his/her whole life. After three short treks, one long Himalayan trek gives a holistic experience of the trekking. Undergoing a tiresome journey along with your colleagues, far from the hustle-bustle of daily life and in the nature's lap, gives a different feeling altogether. In the middle of the trek, we got tired. We started thinking that we would not be able to move forward, but our new friends and zeal enabled us to complete the journey and reach our destination.

The diversity and charisma of the Academy's Foundation Course is matchless. It is the academy's specialty to keep over 350 Officer Trainees of various civil services together and prepare a colorful bouquet of them. It is interesting, as well as astonishing that, despite of such a large number of trainees, one gets acquainted with almost everyone by the time this course of three months ends. Moreover, it is certain that some of the trainees might become close friends with more than a dozen trainees, because each trainee is a part of different groups in various activities, and it is compulsory to take part in all the activities.For example, your lecture group/class will be different from your counselor group;

your trekking group will be different from your village visit group; your hostel mates will be different from the mates of your extracurricular activities; your friends in the language class will be different from the friends in the club or society which you are associated with. Besides, the colleagues of your service and cadre are different; and in the multi-colored and special cultural programme-'India Day', which is organized in the academy every year, the friends of your regional zone too will be different.

The benefit of this diversity is that you meet each and every colleague of yours at some point or the other, and get a chance to talk to everyone at one point or the other. Another good system of the academy is that every Officer Trainee is divided into various counselor groups. The faculty member, chosen as the counselor of each group, meets the group once in two or three weeks. In this meeting, you can share your problems of any sort and the faculty member, i.e., your counselor will try to solve your problem. Thus, a counselor plays the role of your teacher and mentor also.

The structure of the foundation course is such that it keeps the Officer Trainees occupied.Generally, no leave is provided during this period. Even the holidays are spent in doing some activities. The festival of Dussehra comes during this period. Generally, being far away from the home makes you nostalgic, but various creative activities in the academy fill this gap to a certain extent. On the occasion of Dussehra, the 'Hobbies Club' organized many creative activities. The activity of decorating the traditional yet theme -based Rangolis impressed me deeply,e.g., someone portrayed the Goddess Durga in her splendid form, while Lord Ganesha was spreading smiles in others;at one place, peacock was enjoying, and at some other place the lotus was spreading its exquisite beauty; at one place, our festivity was shown through various signs of Dussehra, and at some other place, the interrelationship between the nature and the human being was displayed. Really, our cultural diversity and the inherent unity was expressed uniquely. It is worth mentioning that the creativity of the academy's Officer Trainees was mind blowing.

Moreover, the academy organized various cultural evenings of famous artists from time to time at the Sampoornanand Auditorium, with the objective to develop a sensitivity in the Officer Trainees towards our culture and heritage. Out of these cultural evenings, one was organized on the Sufi music and culture. It was presented by the famous Sufi musical group 'Chaar Yaar'.

For the Officer Trainees of LBSNAA, this evening has been very special and delightful, as we have been completely immersed in the spiritual notes of the four Sufi friends and their musical instruments of the East and the West, i.e., Sarod, Tabla, Harmonium and Guitar. We can never forget these four Sufi friends and their divine music, as they represented the Hindu, Muslim, Sikh and Christian communities as well as the composite culture of India.

They started with the Lord's prayer and spread joy in the environment through their singing. They touched the heart of their listeners by connecting the strings of their divine music with their heart.

The sufi singers of the 'Char Yaar' troupe stirred our souls by reciting the poetry of the 18th century Sufi Saint Baba Bulleshah. The tune of 'Thaiya-Thaiya' was, in fact, the call for the soul's merger into the Supreme Spirit. The fusion of the East and the West, the journey from Rumi to Kabir and the tunes of 'Imagine' resonated in the auditorium, establishing the music's supremacy transcending the geographical boundaries. Kabir,the Sufi Sant, has very well echoed the mysticism of the Sufi tradition in the following couplet:

"Lali mere laal ki, jit dekhun tit laal,
Lali dekhan main gayi, main bhi ho gai laal".

This musical evening was reaching towards its climax with the song 'Damadam mast kalandar'. The listeners were chanting 'Jhoolelal' and were giving rhythm to it by clapping their hands. The four pillars of the Indian Sufi Tradition: Khwaja Moinuddin Chisti, Kutubuddin Kaki, Baba Fareed and Hazrat Nizamuddin Auliya were remembered in the end of the programme by reciting the following mystic expression of Amir Khusrau on the demise of Nizamuddin Auliya, his teacher:

"Gori sove sej par, sir par dale kes,
Chal khusso ghar aapne, rain bhayee chahu des"!

In this manner, the musical evening came to an end with the standing ovation by the faculty members and the Officer Trainees.

Similarly, other cultural evenings were also organized. The major programmes among them were the memorable evening of Carnatic music by the Bombay Jayshree Ramnath and the Folk Dance evening presented by the North-Central Zone Cultural Centre etc. Besides, a cultural evening of the Officer Trainees was also organized during this period. All of us took an active part in it. The evening included drama, dance, singing and various other cultural activities. Watching my colleagues perform, I felt that all of them are so talented. Though the Civil Services preparations are considered to be boring, but the Officer Trainees exhibited their multifaceted talents in this programme. They proved that they could excel not only in the studies but also in the socio-cultural activities. I was fortunate enough to have got the opportunity to host this evening.

We were taken for an educational visit to the 'National Institute for Visually Handicapped' (NIVH) and 'Raphael', an NGO of the mentally challenged children in Dehradun. We were explained the various activities being conducted there. Both the institutions provide good facilities to the handicapped children, and make an effort to educate, train and rehabilitate such children. We too empathized with these children and bought the products made by them. Seeing the brio and courage of these mentally and visually challenged children, I recalled the sayings of Scott Hamilton, the Olympic Gold Medalist athlete, *" only disability in the life is a bad attitude"*.

On the occasion of Gandhi Jayanti, a huge literary festival was organized in the academy. The noted personalities of the literary world, like Ramchandra Guha, Ashok Vajpayee, Mrinal Pandey, Maina Bhagat, Urvashi Butalia, Anuja Chauhan, Anjum Hasan, Shaikh Mahmood, Vikram Sampath, Aftab Seth and Ira Trivedi participated in these events. I was the escort officer of Shri Ashok Vajpayee (In the academy, an Officer Trainee is designated to become the escort officer for every guest and guest speaker who comes there). Fortunately, I got two days to spend with Shri Ashok Vajpayee, the noted poet and critic of Hindi; and I made the maximum utilization of this opportunity. Ashok Vajpayee,a retired I.A.S is quite an interesting personality. No one can get bored in his company, as he keeps narrating the interesting and hilarious stories of the parallel journeys of his administrative and literary life.

In fact, in the literary festival various sessions and programmes were conducted. In the first session, Dr. Saif Mahmood recited the Urdu couplets to make us realize the strength of poetry. Thereafter, various authors presented their views on the topic- 'Maintaining the liveliness of Indian Languages' in a joint session. Apart from this, the authors discussed on their own writings and the process of their creation and also on their favorite books etc. During the evening tea-break, the Officer Trainees bought the books of various authors, and took their autographs on the same. In the evening of the first day of the event, a composite form of Indian Classical Dances- 'Sannidhi' was presented by Parvati Dutta.

On the occasion of Gandhi Jayanti, a homage was paid to Gandhiji and Shastriji through the Bhajans, like *'Raghupati Raghav Raja Ram'* and *'Vaishnav Jan To Tene Kahiye'*. Ramchandra Guha, the noted author, gave a lecture on the topic- 'Relevance of Gandhi and Ambedkar for India'. In order to increase the participation of the Officer Trainees, some interesting workshops were organized on understanding the art forms, clay pottery, Mithila folk painting art, and calligraphy. The grand closing of this literary-cultural festival was done with a poetic evening.

The component of trekking in the lap of Himalaya / NGO Attachment was one of the most important components of the Foundation Course. In it, all the Officer Trainees are divided into different groups, and they are sent to different places of Uttrakhand for trekking. This trekking experience becomes the most memorable experience of the life in the academy.

I find that the knowledge acquired in the lap of nature is not less than the academic knowledge accumulated in our lives. Our one - week NGO Attachment not only developed in us an understanding of the hill life and beauty of nature but also instilled a feeling of compassion for the fellow human beings.

I always used to have a strange eagerness and curiosity in my heart about the beauty of the mountains and the people residing at these places. We usually come here only in the summer vacations for roaming and enjoying the pleasant weather; and after spending four to five days or one week, we return back to our homes keeping in heart the soulful image of the mountains. Moreover,during our tour, we remain so busy in enjoying the weather that we hardly pay attention to the people residing there and their problems.

This journey not only motivated us to understand the difficult life of the people living in the mountains, but also inspired us to seek the resolution of their issues.

In the morning of 3rd October, we started our long journey in a bus from the academy, and left for Gopeshwar (Chamauli District). We passed through Dhanaulti, had brunch in Kaddukhal and then reached Gopeshwar via, Tihri, Shrinagar, Rudraprayag, Karnaprayag and Nandprayag. This bus journey was 12 hours – long, but we converted this boring journey into an interesting one through our multilingual 'Antakshari' in which the songs from the different languages, like Hindi, Tamil, Telugu, Bangla, English and even Spanish were sung. During the journey, we viewed the various dimensions of the beauty of mountains, the ladder- shaped fields and the landslides. In this manner, our day ended, and we reached Gopeshwar (Chamauli).

We spent four days with Sh. Chandi Prasad Bhattji, the winner of 'Gandhi Peace Prize' and 'Ramon Magsaysay Award'.He is a noted Gandhian thinker, environmentalist and social activist, who has spread an awareness towards the environment conservation across the country, including Uttrakhand. During this period, we observed various work done by his organization, namely 'Dashauli Gram Swrajya Mandal'. Here, we observed the working of 'Mahila Mangal Dal' and also participated in its constructive activities being conducted in various villages. We saw the place from where 'Chipko Movement' began, and had a glimpse of afforestation being done in the forests. Besides this, we interacted with the students of the Government Girls Inter College and Degree College.

I was highly impressed by the simple and low-profile persona of Sh. Chandi Prasad Bhattji. The down-to-earth nature of Bhattji, who has been awarded with the 'Padhma Bhausan' award, has amazed us. He leads a simple life; and despite of his old age, he is very active and still possesses a will to do good. It is an inspiration to us. As the parting gift, he gave me a book on his memoirs entitled, 'Parvat-Parvat Basti-Basti'. I wrote a review of that book only after returning to the academy.

The academy's life is interesting because it is full of diversity, i.e., from morning till evening, so many activities take place simultaneously that the officer trainees get accustomed to leading a life full of joy and creativity in stress too. In addition, they study, play games, make friends and fulfill their hobbies/interests as well as keep developing the new skills also. Let us discuss some more aspects of the academy's interesting life.

In the academy, various classes are conducted regularly from morning till evening, and in the end, exams are also conducted. The duration of the foundation course was three and a half months. During the course, we appeared in two mid-term exams; and at the end of the course, we appeared in the final exam. When during the exam days, the academy's environment became stressful,every trainee used to recall the struggling days of UPSC preparations when we studied hard surviving on hot tea only.It is a natural phenomenon, whether you wish or not, stress does crop up during the last days prior to the exam; but due to the pressure, the pace of our reading also increases considerably.

The life of the officer Trainees, during the foundation course,becomes colourful because the Officers Trainee's clubs/ societies fill the vibrant colors in it. As stated earlier that the selection of the Secretary and the members of these societies is done in the first week of the foundation course itself,I got the opportunity to work as the Secretary of the House Journal Society (Literary Society). The work allotted to me was of my interest,therefore I enjoyed it very much. I, along with four other members of the society, published the academy's Monthly News Letter as well as a multilingual collection of self-composed poetry of the Officer Trainees, namely 'Abhivyakti'. At the end of the foundation course, we published a 'Memoir' of about 350 Officer Trainees, in which all the trainees shared their lovely memories of the life with one another during this period. Moreover, we tried to create a conducive environment in the campus for the various literary and creative activities, like Poetry Writing Competition, Short Story Writing Competition, Kavi Sammelan etc. I feel that while working in the society, we not only develop a creative environment for others but also inculcate a team spirit and leadership quality.

The other clubs/societies gave new dimension to the lively campus life by organizing the various interesting activities, especially at the weekends. Any Officer Trainee can take part in the activities of any society. The sports, like cricket, kabbadi, lawn tennis, badminton, squash, tug of war, etc. and activities like giving tuition to the deprived children of the neighborhood, counseling or weekly medical clinic, Nature's photography competition, cultural evenings, exhibition of new and old films, bungee jumping, river rafting, computer- based games, management games and debates on the contemporary issues have made the foundation course very lively and developed a versatility in our personality as well.

The other activities, which have been organized regularly during the last days of the foundation course, are:village visit, fete, athletic meet, shramdan, plays and the cultural programme- 'India Day'.

Let us discuss the village visit. In the academy, the Officer Trainees are sent to the selected villages of India for a week to have a firsthand experience of the actual village life. Generally, an Officer Trainee is sent to a village of the state other than his own home state. I,along with my five other colleagues, got the chance to spend a week in a distant village called 'Churag' in Himachal Pradesh's Mandi district.

In the village, we had a first hand experience of the village life, and got to understand the different problems of the villagers. After visiting most of the areas of the village, we made its map, studied the status of the implementation of Panchayati Raj Institution, Education and Health. We also spread an awareness for the Swatch Bharat Mission.

In our unique journey to the Himachal Pradesh, the 'Devbhoomi', we experienced the wonderful colors of nature and the natural splendor of the villages. One evening, *I wrote a poem, the english version of which I am sharing with you:*

'Let us uncover the layers of our hearts...
The red skies which lie above,
And the light green covers which spread beneath,
The sun setting in the far horizon,
What do they whisper?
Let us uncover the layers of our hearts.

The people whose lives are burdensome,
But they carry smiles on their faces,
The sweetness of those smiles,
We must carry them with us too.
Let us uncover the layers of our hearts.

In the sweet smell of the soil,
Resides every smell of our lives,
Taking each and every grain of this soil,
Let us include sweetness in our lives,
Let us uncover the layers of our hearts.

The sweet warmth of relationships,
The slow noise of desires,
Let us express our inner pains,
Let us smile together and let us keep together.
Let us uncover the layers of our hearts.

I feel, that these people residing in the mountainous villages, who are simple, hard working and self- dependent, inspires us to uncover the layers of our hearts and remain happy. In short, the moments spent in the village became one of the most memorable moments of the foundation course.

After the trek and the village visit, the most memorable programme was the 'India Day'. This programme is held for one day only, but its preparations goes on for weeks. The 'India Day' is the festival of Indian Culture celebrated by the Officer Trainees. This programme is divided into three components,i.e., procession, exhibition and cultural evening. In short, this one- day programme gaves a glimpse of the uniqueness of the Indian culture.

All the Officer Trainees are divided into four zones of India - north, south, east and west. The 'India Day' is celebrated on the Sunday. In the morning, a grand procession of the officer trainees, in which all of them wore the traditional Indian dresses, moved from the academy's gate to the inner campus. They adorned themselves like Maharana Pratap, Shivaji, Rani of Jhansi, Kucchipudi dancers etc. Every zone displayed to their level best the culture of every state of India. The view of all the groups moving ahead while exhibiting their folk dances and traditions, was really unique and unprecedented.

In the afternoon, the cultural aspects of all the four zones were displayed, and in the evening, a zone-wise grand cultural evening was held. There was a healthy competition among the young officers to exhibit the cultural specificity of their own zone. Whether it was the expression of various emotional state of mind through the facial expressions and gestures in the Kucchipudi dance, or the presentation of Kathakali dance, the display of the marriage's tradition of Malabar,the Chhath festival of Bihar, the Chau dance of Orissa,the Rabindra Sangeet of Bengal and the Bamboo dance of Mizoram, each activity spread the varied of colors of the composite culture of India.

The speciality of the 'India Day' is that the varied Indian dishes are served in the Officers' Mess on that day. On a single day, we tasted the delicious foods of the various states of India. In this way, the cultural programme of the 'India Day' became a grand cultural festival.

Another important activity - the Stage Drama was organized in the last days of the foundation course. In this activity, the young officers exhibit their acting and directorial skills through various dramatic presentations. Besides, a grand 'Athletic Meet' was held at the Polo ground in which the various competitions in sports were organized for the whole day. Prior to this, the march-past was held in the morning in which the young officers as well as the mounted young officers took part. In addition to these activities, a voluntary blood camp was organized to teach us how to discharge our social duties. The 'Shramdan' was also organized from time to time to sensitize us towards the dignity of labor.

Various special guests, along with the guest speakers of various subjects and Senior Administrative Officers, visited the academy during the Foundation Course. The list includes the personalities, like Shri E.S.L. Narsimhan, Hon'ble Governor of Telangana; Shri Kiren Rijiju, Hon. Minister of State (Home Affairs); Shri Jayant Sinha, Hon. Minister of State (Finance); Shekhar Gupta, a noted journalist; Ramchandra Guha, an author; Jagdish Khattar and Pratap Bhanu Mehta etc.

In this manner, the first and the most interesting phase of the Academy's Training, i.e., the Foundation Course came to an end. In fact, it is impossible to forget the moments spent with the batch mates in the divine and pristine environment of the academy, like waking up early and doing P.T, reaching the class by literally running, studying together, laughing, talking, roaming, eating, playing, singing, and smiling. I will always remember the Foundation Course because I have learnt so many things for the first time.

This unique course not only sensitized us towards the diverse heritage of our country but also polished every aspect of our personality. It is difficult to count the skills and lessons which we learned knowingly or unknowingly during the training. Today when I look back, I find that a qualitative change in my personality, especially at the level of maturity and personality development. The activities conducted at the academy developed a sensitivity and group dynamics amongst us. We became aware of the unity in the geographical, social,cultural and life of the country amidst the linguistic-cultural,religious,caste and region-based diversity of the country. Simultaneously, we became aware of the challenging aspects and realities of the Indian Administration. I pay my sincere thanks to the respected faculty members and the colleagues for making these moments lively, special and memorable. I wish to conclude my account of the Foundation Course with the following lines of the famous poet Basheer Badr:

"Chiragon ko aankhon me mahfooz rakhna,
badi door tak raat hi raat hogi,
Musafir ho tum bhi, musafir hain hum bhi
Kisi mod par fir mulakat hogi"

"Save my images in your memory,
We may not meet very soon again.
I and you both are travelers,
We may meet at some point of time".

❑❑

Exploring Unity in Diversity: The Bharat Darshan

"Dhoop me niklo, ghataon me nahakar dehko,
Zindagi kya hai, kitabon ko hatakar dekho"

"Go outside in the sun, bathe in the clouds,
If you want to see life, see it by keeping the books aside".

These lines by noted Urdu Poet Nida Fazli always appealed me, but I understood its true essence during our winter study tour, known as the 'Bharat Darshan'.

Our country, India is so diverse, vast and multicolored that one cannot get its holistic view in a limited period of two months. Somehow, we could visit 16 States/ Union Territories of India in our 58- days tour. During this period, we tried to understand the real India and feel its natural, social, cultural, historical, economic, industrial, spiritual specificities. Furthermore, we tried to peep into the heart of the persons living at the extreme end of the country, following the mantra of Gandhiji.

Our India-tour was not only limited to visiting the tourist places or having a glimpse of the nature's beauty, but it was a tour to understand the life and issues of the Indians scattered across the country. It was meant to develop an awareness of the wonderful historical and cultural heritage of the country, to understand the political, administrative,democratic and Panchayati structure of the country and to feel the experiences of the army and paramilitary forces guarding our naval-terrestrial-aerial boundaries. The tour is about experiencing the geographical diversity, including pass, plateau, river, sea and islands, and also the life of country's tribal people and marginalized classes.Not only this, it was also about developing an understanding of the difficulties of the people living in the left wing extremism and Naxal affected areas and understanding the long journey of the country's development in the field of agriculture, industry, power, communication, transportation, rural and urban development and the efforts of the government and the non-government sectors in these fields. We left Mussoorie for the India Tour in the chilly weather of December, 2015.

The first stoppage of our study Tour was Bihar- the land of Buddha and Mahavir. There was a heavy rush at the Patna Railway Station. We kept our luggage in the guest house and came out to roam in the city to learn something new. We observeed the working of NTPC plant situated in the town, tasted Barh's famous sweet 'Lai'and the delicious Litti-Choka, the taste of which still lingers on. On our second day in Patna, we visited the Collectorate premises, police helpline, I.C.A.R and Bihar Power Corporation and learnt new lessons on the administration. At night, we visited the Patna Sahib Gurudwara. The experience of visiting the birth place of Guru Gobind Singh was wonderful.

We also visited Nalanda and Gaya. We travelled from Patna to Nalanda early in the morning. In the foggy weather, our journey was amazing, especially the well maintained roads made the journey marvelous. The visit to Rajgir, the pilgrimage place of Hindus, Buddhists, Jains was really wonderful. It has several cultural sites. We saw the Vishwa Shanti Stupa, Ghora Katora and Ancient Nalanda University. There is a rope-way to reach this Stupa. In fact, it is the oldest rope way of India. We were spellbound after seeing the ruins of Nalanda University and pondered over such a developed education system thousands of years ago. In Nalanda, we also visited the theme park – Pandu Pokhar. At this place, a huge statue of Raja Pandu of the Mahabharata age is situated in the middle of a lake. Next morning, it was the day to visit the famous Jal Mandir situated in Pawapuri, the land of Tirthankar Mahavira's salvation. Jal Mandir was situated in a lake, which was brimming with the innumerable lotus flowers and ducks. The sight was immensely pleasing.

It was a spiritual experience to visit the Mahabodhi Temple located in Bodh Gaya. The meditating Buddha moves every heart towards the ultimate peace. The foreign pilgrims were completely immersed in meditation and self-introspection under the Bodhi Tree. What a divine and wonderful view it was! After visiting the Vishnupad Temple, Bodh Gaya, we left for Jharkhand, the land of minerals.

In Jharkhand, we stayed in LWE affected districts of Latehar and Bokaro. We tried to understand the problems of LWE affected areas in these places. Besides, we have found that there is an infinite scope of tourism and employment in these areas. For this, the only thing required is to link the development of these places with the mainstream. After enjoying the unique sunrise of Netarhat, we reached Bokaro, the steel city. The city has developed immensely because of Bokaro Steel and Thermal Plant. After visiting these states, our view about Bihar and Jharkhand has changed,as both the states have developed considerably.

From Jharkhand, we entered directly into the unseen and untouched heaven of India, i.e., the North-east. In North-east, first of all our army attachment was scheduled. This army attachment started from Dibrugarh and ended at the Arunanchal Pradesh, i.e., till the Indo-China border. It was really a unique experience to live with the soldiers and officers of the Armed Forces and closely observe their life, enthusiasm and emotions. Some of the most memorable moments of our Army attachment are: spending night in a sleeping bag in an extremely chilling weather, patrolling near the riverside in the dark nights, trekking along the dangerous paths on the mountains, practicing the hitting of the target during shooting, going to the border in trucks and trekking up to our Observation Posts. It was the aim of this attachment to make us understand the challenges and the preparations of the army units related with the defence of our country and to sensitize us towards the issues of the soldiers.

After the attachment, we reached Assam's Tinsukia district. On this land of tea estates, the natural beauty is spread all around. We went to Monguri, where we did the boating and got a chance to see the different species of birds very closely.It was an interesting experience. The Digboi's Oil Refinery and Margherita's coal mines suggest that every part of this country plays an important role in the nation-building. We got a chance to see the real beauty of North-east in Meghalaya. Shillong is a very peaceful and beautiful city. It was raining when we reached in Asia's cleanest village, i.e., Mawlynnong. The floating fogs in the way makes us feel that we are among the clouds. Really, the name 'Meghalaya' stands true here. The astonishing 'Living Root Bridge' and the 'Sky Walk' made of the bamboos gave us immense pleasure.

Tripura was the last stoppage in our North-east's journey. I have many memorable experiences of Tripura stored in my heart, like the spectacled monkey of the Clouded Leopard National Park, different species of snakes of North-east in the Snake Show, Tripureshwari Temple and the handicrafts made from the local bamboos. From Tripura, we left for West Bengal directly.

Kolkata, the erstwhile capital of British Empire, still has the remnants of British Rule. The Victoria Memorial tells the tale of British Rule in India. The Dakshineshwari and Kalighat temples in a city, which are world famous for Durga Puja, filled us with the feeling of an immense devotion towards the Goddess Durga. The Howrah Bridge,the life line of Kolkata, leaves you mesmerized; and the tea, gossips and Park Street's beauty has made us fall in love with this place. Really, Kolkata is the cultural capital of India and is the true 'city of joy'. Here, we visited the 'Garden Reach Ship Builders Ltd.' and celebrated the Republic Day too. After seeing the grand Republic Day Parade, we reached the Andaman and Nicobar islands, located in the distant south-east. As soon as we landed at the Port Blair Airport, we encountered an extreme hot and humid weather. The light and sound show of the Cellular Jail displayed the tortures during Kala-Pani's punishment, which used to be given to the revolutionaries during the British rule. In Andaman, our Naval and Coast Guard attachment was scheduled. It was quite a unique experience to comprehend the attentiveness and problems faced by our Navy officers while in a Navy ship. The coast guards were working with full dedication while guarding the Indian Coasts.

We went to Havlock to understand the geographical conditions of the island and the lives of the people residing there. We did scuba diving and enjoyed a lot on Radhanagar and Kala Patthar beaches. We enjoyed so much that we were not willing to leave that place. I can never forget the scooter ride till Radhanagar, especially the sweet breeze that came from the coconut trees situated on both sides of the road. The exemplary mutual harmony among the people of the Andaman-Nicobar Islands presents a model before the whole nation, as there is no communal or linguistic tension there. Hindi is the link language of this place and various multi-lingual persons use Hindi with ease.

After Andaman, we visited the South India. Chennai is a big city which is culturally very rich. In Chennai,the roads, food and the its heritage is commendable.The Government Museum and Court Museum, Marina Beach and Vivekananda House, Kapaleshwar and Parthasarthi Temples are the witnesses of Tamilnadu's historical and cultural heritage. You must visit the South India to see the fine architecture of the temples. Here, we also visited the premises of some private sector companies, like Ashok Leyland, T.V.S and Central Leather Research Institute. I was always very fond of the south-indian food, hence during our stay in South, I never asked for the North-Indian food.

From Tamilnadu, we left for Karnataka. Though Bengaluru is a well organized and attractive city, but there is a huge traffic problem here. It is an I.T. Hub. We visited the Science and Technology Museum and the Lal Bagh Botanical Garden. The architecture of the Karnataka Assembly Building is mesmerizing. The inscription - 'Government work is God's work' on the assembly building's main gate always motivates us to remain dedicated to our service. We visited the Akshay Patra Foundation and tried to understand its selfless role in the implementation of Mid-Day Meal Scheme across the country. We also visited the premises of 'Janagraha Centre for Citizenship and Democracy' and Narayan Hridalaya.

Thereon, we moved towards the twin city of Sikandrabad-Hyderabad. The idol of Blessing Buddha, situated in the Hussain Sagar Lake, looked enticing. Charminar is the pride of this city. If you have not seen the beauty of Charminar's market, then you really missed something in your life. In Hyderabad, our Air Force Attachment was scheduled. We visited the College of Air Warfare, Navigation Training School and the grand Air Force Academy and tried to understand the simulator, night vision, aero-medicine and the manner in which the flight of airplanes are conducted and controlled. The Indian Air Force, with the mantra of *'Touch the sky with glory'*, continues to touch the new heights. In Hyderabad, we also visited the premises of 'Centre for Cellular and Molecular Biology' which is a C.S.I.R. centre.

Our next stoppage was Bhadrachalam (Khammam) in Telangana. It is the major site of Shri Ram's route for His Forest Stay, so it is a big pilgrimage centre. Our Temple Trust Management Attachment was scheduled at Bhadrachalam. We visited the Bhadrachalam Temple as well as the Parnashala which had witnessed the Forest Stay of Shri Ram, Laxman and Sita.We physically entered into the coal mines of Singreni to understand the process of coal mining. Khammam district is a Naxal affected district. We went to the tribal areas and analyzed the ongoing efforts of the government in the field of Education and Health. Besides, we also had a face-to-face interaction with the rural women and female students.

After this memorable journey of South India, we reached Nagpur- the city of oranges. We visited the Multi-Modal International Cargo Hub and Airport (MIHAN) and Manganese Ore India limited (MOIL)and tried to understand the story behind their industrial development. Then, we left for Chindwara, Madhya Pradesh. We learned the work-culture of the newly established Municipal Corporation through the meaningful discussions with their public representatives. From here, we went to Delhi and visited the National Security Guard and the National Disaster Response Force.

It is not an exaggeration if I say that these two months of the Bharat Darshan Tour are the most memorable days of my life. Many things happened for the first time in my life. I learnt the new lessons and developed a consciousness, sensibility and sensitivity towards the various issues of our society and nation. The unity in diversity, explored during the India Tour, touched me and matured me as well; and it will remain in my heart forever. How aptly Ismael Merathi has said in the following lines:

"Sair kar duniya ki gafil, zindgani fir kahan,
Zindgani gar rahi to, naujawani fir kahan."

"O negligent man! Travel the world as there is only one life,
Even if you live for long, you will not remain young forever".

❑❑

Rajasthan Darshan: Exploring Rajasthan in Monsoon

I, along with seven other Officer Trainees, left for this memorable eighteen - days road journey by a tempo traveller. When the driver saw our huge bags, he commented, "only the Indian tourists carry such bags;otherwise, the entire luggage kept in a car by the foreign tourists is equal to the luggage of a single Indian traveler"!

Well, with this innocent but interesting comment of the driver, we left Jaipur for Bikaner. The landscape kept on changing gradually, as we moved ahead on our way. The roads were well-maintained, so despite of it being a long distance journey, the distance did not appear much. The Circuit House in Bikaner is immensely beautiful; it gives a feeling of the royalty. In the morning, we reached Lalgarh.The Lalgarh Fort is the new fort of Bikaner' Royal Family,where they reside in one portion of it. The Laxmi Niwas Palace is situated in the Lalgarh Fort premises. The Lalgarh Fort narrates the glory of Bikaner's royal lineage. The fort has a gold-plated room with the golden engravings on its walls.

Afterwards, we went to Junagarh, the oldest fort in Bikaner. This Royal Fort was established in 1948; and no intruder has ever been able to capture this fort. The Phool Palace, Badal Palace and Darbar Hall are the pride of this fort. There are interesting stories about the Badal Palace,e.g., it seldom rains in Bikaner.So, whenever it rained, the prince got scared. In order to allay his fear, a palace was built in which the actual painting of the clouds, thunder and rain were painted; and in this manner, the children of the royal family were mentally prepared for the rains.

If you ever get a chance to visit Bikaner, then you must go to the Sate Archives, one of the best archives of the country. We can learn the art of maintaining and preserving our heritage and historical documents from the Rajasthan. While roaming around in the evening we reached the Jail Road. Here, we got an opportunity to taste the famous Sharbat of Chunnilal Tanwar. We had the Sharbat of Jasmine, White rose and Dry coriander. There are some old Havelies in the old areas of Bikaner City. These havelies are palacial, beautiful and grand. One must visit the Rampuria Haveli. After visiting these glorious havelies, I was reminded of the architectural magnificence of the buildings in the old cities of Europe.

We visited the world famous Karni Mata's Temple situated at Deshnok. There were innumerous rats inside the temple, called as 'Kaba'.Amazingly,the rats inside the temple never leave it, and the rats outside the temple never enter it. Generally, these rats remain asleep and do not hurt anyone. There are four to five white rats here, and it is considered to be a good omen if you happen to see them. From Bikaner, we visited Nokha,and had lunch in Nagaur. There is no dearth of greenery in Rajasthan. Generally, we associate Rajasthan with the deserts, but in reality, there is no sand in most of the districts of Rajasthan.

The next day, we reached the Blue City- Jodhpur. Here, we visited the famous Mehrangarh Fort. It was built in 1459, and the last construction was done in the year 1808. There are seven gates in the fort, including the Jai Pole and Fateh Pole. From the fort's top, one can get a splendid view of the blue city. Jodhpur appears blue from the Mehrangarh fort, as Jaipur appears pink from the Nahargarh fort. The war tanks are exhibited at the top of the fort. The fort appears to be a fusion of the Hindu-Muslim Art. The golden Palki, brought from Ahmadabad, and Akbar's sword are the specialties of this fort. It is the uniqueness of Rajasthan that each fort surpasses the other fort in terms of beauty, architecture and grandeur.

After Mehrangarh, we reached the Umed Bhawan Palace, which is considered to be the best hotel in India. This huge residential building was built in the 20th century, and presently, it hosts the residence of the current king and a hotel too. This exemplary palace exudes the royal grandeur. In the evening, we bought the special namkeens of Jodhpur.

The next morning, we left Jodhpur for Jaisalmer. Our first stoppage was Osiya, a place considered to be the place of origin of the people of Oswal caste, who are scattered across the country. The 2500 years old temple complex is dedicated to the four communities:Shaiva, Vaishnava, Shakta and Jain. This temple is built from the stones, in which the Limestone has not been used at all in its construction. In the whole city of Osiya, there are temples everywhere, and some very ancient temples are built from the red stone also.

It feels very comfortable and safe to travel by road in Rajasthan. In addition, the journey by road provides you a glimpse of the geography and life of Rajasthan. We were able to view the dust - filled clouds even before reaching Ramdevra and Pokhran. It is common to see the dust - filled winds here. Generally, the traffic was not much on the roads in Rajasthan, but it became less when we travelled towards the Western Rajasthan. We reached the tomb of Baba Ramdev, a spiritual Guru of the fifteenth century.

In his time, the Baba opposed the practice of casteism and untouchability. The Ramsarovar lake, situated at this place, keeps drying up within a few days. During the monsoon season, a big fare is organized here. Mostly, all the shops near the temple sell the decorated fabric horses.

It had started raining slowly, when we reached a wonderful place called Bhadriyaji. In Bhadriyaji, there is a big library and a huge cow shelter of about 25000 cow lineages. In this shelter, there are cows of Tharpar breed who can give milk in 50 degree as well as in -2 degree temperature. The cows run towards the staff of the cow shelter on a single call, like the Narayani Sena reacts on the call of Lord Shri Krishna. The place has a temple of Goddess Durga, where Shree Harbans Singhji Nirmal (Bhadriyaji Maharaj), a Punjabi saint, came to save the shelter-less cows. Babaji used to offer Lassi to the visitors who came to meet him. Therefore, the tradition of offering Lassi is still maintained here. The delicious food ('Prasad')was sheer ambrosia!

Here, we found the names of the places quite interesting. We reached Jaislamer by passing through the places named as 'Baap', 'Chacha' and 'Lathi'etc. Interestingly, when we reached Bikaner and Jaipur, it was raining and when we reached Jailsamer, it rained heavily there as well.

Jaisalmer is known as 'the Golden City' because the yellow stones have been used in the construction buildings in this city. Besides, it is also known as 'the city of windows'. The famous Patwa Haveli, built in the nineteenth century, is situated in Jaisalmer. Here, we saw the special stone called 'sandstone'. The specialty of sandstone is that it becomes soft like wood, if immersed in water for half an hour. Here the Jain temples are very famous. They reminded us of the Jain temples of Dilwara. The beauty of the golden city can be viewed from the Jaisalmer Fort.

After visiting the Jaisalmer Fort, we left for Kuldhara. This ruined village of Kuldhara was a big centre of business; and it existed there since the establishment of Jaisalmer. Many centuries ago, the people of the Paliwal Brahman Kuldhar caste left their own village for Pali due to the atrocities of the then Minister. Here we also saw the structure of a house built then, which contained many water-wells. One of these wells is 80 - feet deep and has ladders too. There used to be a small pillar known as 'Govardhan'.

The same night, we visited a place called 'Sam', where we encountered the sand dunes for the first time in our lives. Whatever we have studied about it, in our school or college days, does not match with the exalted experience of the sand dunes in reality. The view of sand dunes, with drops of rain on it, makes a stupendous view. We were delighted to see a caravan of the decorated camels passing through these sand dunes. We moved far inside the sand dune area. The camel ride was started in 'Sam' a few years ago only. We enjoyed the ride a lot.

In the morning, we left Jaisalmer for Barmer. In this desert, there are high and low roads at various places; and crossing such roads gives a different feeling altogether. You cannot enjoy so much in the rail or air journey, as you do on theses roads. The view of the flocks of sheep and goats grazing alongside the road,the high wind-mills on both sides of the road mesmerized us. It started raining before we reached Barmer. Wherever we went, it rained as if the monsoon was following us.

Barmer is a city of small towns. The life here resembles the life of a town. It is not as advanced as that of the city's life. The 'Kiradu', known as the 'Khajuraho' of Rajasthan, is located near Barmer.

From Barmer, we left directly for Mount Abu. During this journey,we realized that all the shops on the way were named after the names of Gods and Goddesses, like Balaji, Karni Mata, Baba Ramdev and Hanuman. It shows a deep devotion of the Rajasthani people towards their religion. We reached the Abu Road via Sanchor and Raniwada. On the way to the Abu road, the mountains were peeping through the greenery. Such a scenic contrast made an illusion of the mountainous state of 'Meghalaya'. The heavy rains made the environment heavenly and divine. The journey of 27 kms from the Abu Road to the Mount Abu was an unforgettable experience. It reminded us of the trekking days in Lal Bahadur Shastri Academy, Mussoorie.

The Circuit houses of both the Rajasthan and Gujarat states are located in Mount Abu. Mount Abu is the favorite destination of Gujaratis. The sign boards in the Gujrati language and the tourists conversing in Gujarati was a common sight here. In the evening, we walked up to the Nakki Lakeand viewed the beauty of this Lake by taking a round of it. We also did the boating.

In the morning, we visited the world famous Jain Temples of Dilwara. These temples,the unique monuments of Indian Art and Culture, were built in the eleventh century by Vimalshah. The temple premises is made of the white marbles and comprises five temples. The 'Vimal Vasahi' is dedicated to Lord Adinath. In the circumambulation path of the temple, there is a roof over every Tirthankar's idol which consists of 125 square blocks.Amazingly, the craftsmanship and design of each block is different. The various myths from Indian Mythology have been uniquely portrayed in these images. The Loonvasahi Temple is dedicated to the Tirthankar Neminath; and there are two caricatures of Devrani and Jethani in the temple. The wives of the constructor of this temple, Vashtupal and Tejpal, wanted to be remembered for centuries. So, both of them borrowed money from their respective fathers and made two caricatures. There is a minor difference between these two caricatures and one fails to differentiate between them in a glance.

The international headquarter of the 'Brahmkumaris', a spiritual organization, is situated in Mount Abu and provides the training of 'Rajyoga'. Thousands of its followers throng this place, wearing white clothes. We returned from Mount Abu and left for Udaipur. We reached Udaipur via N.H. 27. We felt quite relaxed on the way, as there was a greenery on both the sides of the road. The red-golden stones on both the sides of the road and the dense greenery in between looked very beautiful. There is a place called 'Kavita', which is located just before the Udaipur city.

On the way, we visited Ranakpur's Jain Temple, which comprises 1,444 pillars.It is a unique example of architecture. After this, we visited the Kumbhalgarh Fort, which is the biggest fort of India. Interestingly, you cannot locate its existence until you reach very close to the fort. Because of this reason the invaders, who came to invade this fort, failed to locate it and returned back. The 'Light and Sound Show', organized in the fort, beautifully presents its history.

During our Udaipur visit, I was very much mesmerized by the City Palace. This 1 k.m. long palace is the second largest palace of India. King Uday Singh started the construction of this palace in the year 1559,and his successors completed its construction in about 400 years. The large gates of the place are known as 'Pol', and the small gates are known as 'Dyodhi'. Our guide told us an interesting fact that the small gates were built so that the invaders would face difficulty in entering the palace. Besides, we also saw the 'Saheliyon ki Bari' and 'Moti Magri'. In 'Saheliyon ki Bari', the queens used to come for recreation. Moti Magri is the tomb dedicated to Maharana Pratap. During our Udaipur stay, we also visited Eklingji and Lord of the Ranas. Besides, we were fortunate enough to have got the opportunity to visit the famous Nathdwara Temple. At night, we visited the Jagmandir Palace situated in the middle of Pichola Lake. The scenery and environment of the Jagmandir Palace in the middle of Pichola Lake is wonderful. I heard the tune of the musical instrument 'Jal Tarang' for the first time in my life at the palace itself.

From Udaipur, we left for Banswara in the morning. On the was, there was greenery and vast mountainous ranges. What a ride it was! We reached Banswara by crossing several beautiful paths. This district, inhabited by the tribal people, is quite a fascinating place. The Bhil caste and the people from various parts of the country also live here. When Mahi Dam was being built, people from across the nation, especially from South India, came and settled down here. An interesting fact is that the sales of motorcycle are very high in this district. The tribal people love to purchase bikes, despite of their poverty. We had lunch there and left for the Mahi Dam. It is a huge dam and its glaciers are larger than the glaciers of the other dams of the country. We spent quite some time on the dam.

The next day we left for Chachakota from Banswara city. The Chachakota has the extremely beautiful greenery dunes, as Jaisalmer has the sand dunes. Really wonderful! The nature has blessed this place with a bountiful beauty and divinity. It is not an exaggeration, Banswara is the Switzerland of India.Roaming freely at the high and low grassland spread across the Aravali in Chachakota, is a great pleasure of life. A photographer in you would feel elated while being at this place. Really, the punchline of Rajasthan